THE PIANO

By
Wanda J. Scott

Elverah,
Release the music that is flowing on the inside of you!

Wanda J. Scott

Copyright © 2021 by Wanda J. Scott.

Library of Congress Control Number   2021906840
ISBN: Softcover   978-1-950425-33-4
            eBook   978-1-950425-35-8

Cover and Title Page by Rebekah Legault

All rights reserved solely by the author. The author guarantees all contents are original and do not infringe upon the legal rights of any other person or work. No part of this book may be reproduced in any form without the permission of the author.

This book is sold subject to the condition that it shall not, by way of trade or otherwise, be lent, re-sold, hired out or otherwise circulated without the author's prior consent in any form of binding or cover other than that in which it is published and without a similar condition including this condition being imposed on the subsequent purchaser.

Published in the United States of America.

Liber Publishing House
www.liberpublishing.com
Hotline: 718 577 1006

Quantity sales. Special discounts are available on quantity purchases by corporations, associations, and others. For details, contact the publisher at above information.

DEDICATION

I am truly blessed by my best friend, mentor, and loving husband Don, who has encouraged me in my writing for the past 33 years. It was his encouragement and prayers that has brought me to this place in my writing. He has been there in my balcony, cheering me on to the finish line. This has been a joint effort of my writing and his dedication to edit and format every page.

And to my oldest sister Pat Knight, who encouraged me to keep going and also edited my work.

CHAPTER 1

"Not again!" Nicole shouted, as she read the note her mother had posted on the front of the refrigerator, dinner will be late. Devin's soccer game is at four, I will pick up something for your dinner on the way home, your father and I have a dinner meeting at seven.

Scooping Snowball, her white angora cat, up in her arms Nicole ran upstairs to her room. Flinging herself on her bed, beating the pillows with her fist, "why? Why?" she screamed. "My brother can participate in every sport he wants to, not only in school but also in a year-round soccer club. But the one thing that is the desire of my heart, my dream, is treated like a hoax that will cast a bewitching spell on our family.

Since she was ten years old Nicole's dream was to have her very own black ebony baby grand piano and become a concert pianist. This dream has been shattered by her father's refusal to allow music instruments in the house. Without a piano her dream was unreachable.

"A piano is much less expensive than all those expensive gifts and vacations, he lavishes on us" She sobbed burring her face in Snowball's fur. "Music lessons would cost less than all the fees associated with Devin's sports. This dinner tonight, hob-knobbing with the elite will cost more than a month of piano lessons."

Every time Nicole approached the subject of music, her father would immediately suggest she take an interest in gymnastics, soccer, or dance.

Sports held no interest for her. Music was her passion. It is the voice of life, the birds, the trees, and the mountains. *The empty place in me can never be filled with anything else,*

She cuddled Snowball in her arms and sobbed into her pillow and pulling it over her face.

For as long as Nicole could remember her mother's harp had never been a part of the regular furnishings of their house. It stands in the third-floor studio like, a ghost, covered with a sheet. Sometimes when her father is away on business trips, Nicole would hear her mother playing it. *I wonder if she knew Daddy didn't allow musical instruments in the house before she married him. Was her love for him greater than her love for her music?*

Once I heard someone say memories are the stories a family writes together. The story of this family would be an ugly one.

A successful father, who as a young man had climbed the corporate ladder of success very quickly, a mother who obediently attends every activity and performs every duty required of the wife of a successful businessman, laying aside her own desires to be a real person, a son who is an all-star soccer player and an all-state track star and then there's me, a sixteen -year -old angry teenage daughter, who's only desire is to become a concert pianist.

Devin has made him proud; sports are a man thing, but why does he hate his daughter's music talent so much?

Maybe my father never wanted a daughter.

Feeling the ache of rejection ripple through her she commanded herself to put aside the thoughts of her father's rejection of her desire to have a piano and music lessons. *It is not me he is rejecting; it is the music.* She comforted herself.

Nicole put her headphones on and let Chopin's Nocturne immerse her mind. She had listened repetitively to this arrangement until it had become ingrained in her mind and rang in her spirit waiting to escape her fingertips onto the piano keys. Nicole's extra ordinary music talent to play by ear was a gift.

She turned her attention to her music homework assignment, to profile a successful musician. She had chosen Madam Maxine, her favorite concert pianist who had been featured with symphonies and in concerts on New York stages for more than twenty years. Madam Maxine had become Nicole's idol.

Little was known about her personal life, she was born in Pittsburgh, Pennsylvania, went to New York where she struggled for a few years before being discovered by an agent who gave her a start on the big stage. In all the articles about Madam Maxine there was no reference to her last name. She was simply Madam Maxine.

Nicole let her mind drift. *In a few weeks, school will be finished and then I will spend four weeks in Pittsburgh with Aunt Kathryn. Devin will be at the lake with our cousins for two weeks and then at soccer camp for two weeks, while our parents are on an extended European vacation. Always before they took their vacation during the school year. I'm so glad they are doing it during our summer vacation, and I can spend this time with Aunt Kathryn. She understands my love for music.*

"Hey, Nicole!" Devin shouted banging on her bedroom door. "We won our soccer game against the best team in the league,"

Little brothers can be so annoying. "That's cool," Nicole replied halfheartedly. *Why can't my father recognize my love for music like he does my brother's love for soccer?*

Nicole turned her attention back to her homework assignment. Madam Maxine will be conducting a Children's Music Forum in Pittsburgh and Aunt Kathryn had registered Nicole to participate in it.

Just a few more weeks of school and then I will be in Pittsburgh with Aunt Kathryn and hopefully get a chance to meet Madam Maxine. To perform in her presence will be a dream come true.

In reaction to her father's refusal to allow a piano in the house, Nicole's determination to become a good pianist grew stronger than ever. She swore that she would seize every opportunity to lay her fingers on the keys every time she was near a piano until she had accomplished her dream.

Nicole collected her books and tomorrow's homework, put them in her backpack, cuddling Snowball in her arms she drifted off to sleep.

The morning brought the usual anxiety of facing the belligerent mocking of her classmates, she decided to rise above all the anger this created in her.

"This school year will be over in a few more weeks. I can choose what this day will be like and make it happen." She told herself gulping down a glass of orange juice and grabbing a pop tart on the way out the door.

"Devin!" Nicole shouted, "if you are going to ride to school with me get a move on, I'm not going to be late because of your dilly-dallying around."

The first period gym class was her most dreaded class of the day.

In the locker room the girl's voices were like the deep notes at the lower end of the keyboard on a piano that was out of tune.

Nicole's quiet, polite spirit made her different from the loud boisterous personalities of the other girls in the class.

They were jealous of her beauty. Her hair, her skin and her nails were that of a model.

"How could someone love music so much that they exclude themselves from all other school activities?" One of the girls spoke loud enough to make sure Nicole heard.

Today I will rise above all of this, Nicole thought. *I am stronger than their hurtful words, their glares, and those hateful gestures.*

Her music was the outlet she used to release her pain and hurt. *I will accomplish my passion.* Yet the words sometimes made her feel inadequate, insecure, and made her question how she could accomplish her passion without a piano.

THE PIANO

The school music lab was Nicole's happy place. There she escaped those cruel words from this morning's gym class as she sunk into her music and devised a plan to stay on track to prepare for the Children's Music Forum. At first, she started banging on the keys getting louder with each octave to release the frustration welling up on the inside of her and then glided into Ave Maria. Although she didn't know many of the words, the melody soothed her anger and calmed her spirit. Peace flowed over her as she played Chopin's arrangement of Nocturne. *Music is the expression of the joy within me.*

As Nicole lost herself in her music the events of this morning's gym class faded into the distance. At the piano, her dream center was awakened by her music to pursue her dream. She could dream of what it would be like to perform in the presence of Madam Maxine. The icing on the cake would be to actually meet her.

Having her driver's license has enabled Nicole more time to practice her music in the school's music lab while she waits for her brother to finish track practice.

The love for the piano was a consuming fire in her soul and it could block out everything around her. It was her joy and she hoped someday it would become her life.

The rhythm of the music was still moving her as she finished her practice.

She threw her backpack in the back seat of her car and headed to the track. *Practice should be over by now,* she thought.

At breakfast, the next morning Devin excitedly relayed every detail of the upcoming soccer tournament. Nicole dreaded another day of listening to her fellow classmate's tales of how they escape the drudgery of student life through drinking and misadventures. *Just a few more weeks and this will be over.* This year in public school was so different from the private school she had attended in her previous nine years in school, where learning and growing intellectually was her full-time aim. Transferring to public school had sounded so perfect.

"Hey! Nicole, we're going over to Sandy's Ice Cream Parlor why don't you come and hang out with us, one of the guys shouted as her last period class was dismissed?"

"I can't, I must practice my music."

"Why doesn't your old man get you your own piano?" The boy with the long ugly hair, replied. "It would give you more time at home to devote to your music, then you could hang out with us."

Nicole grabbed her backpack and ran from the room. *I must take advantage of every moment I can in the school's music lab to perfect my presentation for the Children's Music Forum. If I get to the lab early maybe I will get to practice on the baby grand piano today.*

Like an angry mob a group of students approached the piano where Nicole was practicing. "Can you make us sound like a tune on your piano?" Richard asked, with a smirk on his face.

Nicole felt the anger rise- up on the inside of her. "Certainly," She replied.

With a thump she pounced on the lowest octave of the keyboard. "That is, you!" Letting her fingers flow two octaves below middle C, "that is Coty," and then flowing three octaves above middle C, "that is Michelle."

What are you doing? She questioned herself, swiftly running her fingers up and down the keyboard octave after octave, "this is your gang of angry student's hell bent on making other's lives miserable."

Nicole quietly flowed into Braham's lullaby, "and this is me, Goodnight!" she shouted and ran from the room and quickly retreated to her car.

The sting of rejection lingered in the air as tears streamed down her face, I *want to make friends but not with bullies, and students that drink and skip school.*

"*How* can anyone be so obsessed and saturated with music that they don't participate in any other school activities or hang out with the gang?" Coty questioned.

THE PIANO

"It's no different than you and your sports," Veronica replied.

"At least I attend the games and interact with the team."

"She comes from a rich family, maybe she thinks she is too good to associate with us." Michelle said.

"I think she's lonely and the piano is her best friend." Veronica added. "She is in all accelerated classes maybe all she does is study."

"If her family is so rich why doesn't she have her own piano?" Richard asked.

"Speaking of studying I have an English exam tomorrow." Coty said. "I hate English, but I need to ace this exam in order to stay on the track team."

"I have a couple of exams also," Michelle said, slinging her backpack over her shoulder.

Nicole entered the empty house; her parents and Devin had already gone to the state soccer tournament. Thank God, studying for my exams next week has exempted me from the family rule that all family members show support by attending each other's activities. *That rule seems to apply to everything except music.* She thought as she scooped up Snowball and buried her face in his fur. This weekend it is just me and you Snowball.

CHAPTER 2

After the hectic schedule of exams, ending the school year and getting ready for her trip, Nicole felt like her life had hit the pause button. With all of that behind her, she pondered what the weeks ahead had in store for her. She laid her suitcase on the bed and started sorting through the clothes she would need for her trip to Aunt Kathryn's. *There's no need to take enough clothes for the whole summer, I'm sure Aunt Kathryn and I will be going on many shopping excursions.*

For whatever reason Aunt Kathryn, a pediatrician, had never married and doted lavishly on Nicole and her brother Devin. She and Nicole share the love of music as well as a deep love for each other.

Aunt Kathryn is the one person who understands my passion for music, Nicole thought. *With her I can express what music and the possibility of meeting Madam Maxine means to me.*

Nicole's excitement was blemished by the sudden thought that gripped her. *For the next four weeks my family will all be living in separate locations, doing different things.*

Devin would be at the lake and soccer camp, Mom and Daddy traveling across Europe and me in my dream world of being able to play Aunt Kathryn's baby grand piano for as many hours a day as I desire.

She had never been away from her parents and brother for that long. Although her brother could be a pain at times, she was going to miss him. And my parents, m*aybe I have just taken them too much for granted. They've always just been here for whatever Devin and I needed.*

THE PIANO

This will be an extra special dinner tonight. I will not bring up the subject of music. I will not let them know how disappointed I am with my life, but I certainly will let them know how much I love them.

Nicole carefully chose one of her father's favorite outfits and placed the aquamarine ring he had given her for her sixteenth birthday, on her finger.

Daddy seemed extra quiet as they entered the restaurant where all their special occasions were celebrated; birthdays, Nicole's nineth grade graduation, Devin's state track championship and mother's win of the women's state amateur tennis tournament, but tonight is different. In a few days we will all be going in different directions.

As they pondered the menu choices, Daddy cleared his throat. Nicole detected an excitement in his voice as he announced, "The offer to move the company from overseas back to the states has been accepted."

Her mind shifted to speed dial. What she thought was just a vacation was really a business trip. That's why they changed their trip from during the school year to now. This will change the course of all our lives. Another move, another new school, maybe even another state.

Nicole had always been independent, but another reset for her life was frightening. Having to make another adjustment was scary.

Her mind flashed back to their last move. She was still struggling to make friends. Coming from private school to public school, her interest was so different, and her education level was much higher. Having no interest in sports made her a target for the pranks and criticism of her classmates.

"Instead of moving it means I will have to do a lot of traveling." He continued, "it won't be the ideal life, but it will be better than disrupting all our lives and moving to another state or another country."

Relief flowed through Nicole. *Thank God not another new school or new city to get used to.*

"I will arrange my schedule so that I'm home for all of our special events and holidays."

I guess that doesn't include me I don't have any special events because that doesn't include music. Nicole pondered.

"It is going to be hard for all of us being apart for the next four weeks, I hope I can wrap up all the details and get this project finished sooner. The one thing I need to know is if we are all in agreement as a family, that this is the best option for all of us."

"We've arranged a busy summer for both of you so the time will pass more quickly." Victoria said. "We' re going to miss you terribly but we think this is the best solution for the situation."

Devin sat quietly contemplating what had just been discuss. He loved being at the lake with his cousins and soccer was his passion but four weeks without his family was something he had never experienced.

The lump in Nicole's throat kept her from speaking. *Not having my family will be worse than not having a piano. But this is only for four weeks.*

"I'm in," Nicole answered.

"Me too," Devin echoed.

Back home the hub of activity centered on coordinating everyone's schedules.

Getting Devin to meet up with his cousins to go to the lake, overlapped with Nicole's time to be at the airport. She convinced her parents, John, and Victoria, that at sixteen she was mature and responsible enough to make the trip from Charlotte, NC to Pittsburgh, PA. by herself.

The busy airport was nothing new to Nicole. She had accompanied her father on many business trips and waited out many schedule delays.

THE PIANO

But traveling alone was a first for her and made her feel mature and important.

She placed her ticket on the counter, her long fingers displayed perfectly manicured nails, the large aquamarine ring her father had given her for her sixteenth birthday glittered under the lights. *If only he could realize a piano is much more important to me than expensive jewelry,* she thought.

"What beautiful nails," the counter clerk said. Are they sculptured nails?"

Nicole thought for a moment. "No," she replied, "they are my own." And politely thanked the clerk.

Still looking at those beautiful hands the perfect manicured nails, and the glitter of the aquamarine ring. "You must be a piano player," the clerk said handing Nicole her boarding pass.

"I'm on my way to Pittsburgh, PA to participate in a Music Forum."

"Your plane boards at gate 41."

Nicole placed her boarding pass in the side pocket of her music portfolio and entered the concourse leading to gate 41.

Holding her hands out in front of her, "what are sculptured nails?" She asked herself. "If I don't know what they are I guess I don't have them." She did not see the young man running towards her until they collided. Sheets of music fell from the unzipped pocket of her music portfolio.

The young man's hand stopped in mid- air as he handed her the sheets of music, he had retrieved. Her deep brown eyes were deep enough to swim in and the astonished look on her face was as cute as a kitten trying to catch a butterfly.

A smile touched his lips. "Hi, I'm Kevin. Are you a pianist?"

Nicole reached for the music Kevin was holding. "Ah, Ah, yes I am, I'm Nicole, my flight leaves in forty -five minutes." She replied, her eyes still glued to his. She quickly placed the sheets of music in her portfolio.

Nicole checked the flight schedule; her flight was on time which allowed her enough time to dash into the restroom and make a last minute check of her hair and makeup. Her olive skin with a touch of blush, long dark lashes, framed by coal black wavy hair, gave her the look of a model. She had been asked many times why she didn't apply for a modeling job at one of the local department stores, but her only interest was music.

She was so focused on The Children's Music Forum sponsored by Madam Maxine, that until now she had not been unaware of the knot in her stomach. Was it the anticipation of performing in the presence of and the possibility of meeting Madam Maxine or the fact she hadn't told her parents the real reason she wanted to spend a month with Aunt Kathryn instead of accompanying then on their European trip?

Determined to not let anything interfere with the excitement of spending time with Aunt Kathryn and enjoying the art and music culture of Pittsburgh, Nicole took out her boarding pass. She straightened her shoulders, held her head high and boarded the plane. Row one seat B, *perfect a window seat.* As she settled into her seat a grey-haired lady tapped her on the shoulder, "excuse me," she said, "you're in my seat."

Nicole looked at her boarding pass. "It says row one seat B."

"It must be over there." The lady replied, pointing to the other side of the aisle.

Nicole secured her portfolio and moved to the other side of the plane.

"Sorry miss that is my seat," said a deep male voice.

The flight attendant looked at Nicole's boarding pass. "Honey that flight left fifteen minutes ago." She said, "this flight is full."

"My ticket said flight 304, departure time eleven AM." Suddenly Nicole didn't feel grown up at all.

THE PIANO

"Just wait right here," the flight attendant said. "I'll be back in a minute."

The flight attendant came toward her smiling. "We have an empty seat. in row three and one in the back of the plane."

Nicole turned to take the seat in row three, the passenger in the aisle seat rose to let her pass, their eyes met. "Kevin!" she exclaimed. Nicole settled back in her seat. *I can't believe I am sitting next to the person that nearly ran me down earlier.*

Kevin, noticing the black music portfolio asked, "Are you performing in Pittsburgh?"

"I am participating in a Children's Music Forum sponsored by the Famous Pianist, Madam Maxine. And your mission is?"

"I'm a member of the National Eagle's Soccer Club. We are competing in Pittsburgh to raise money for the Children's Hospital Cancer Center. Then I'm going to spend a couple of weeks with my grandmother."

Nicole let her mind mull over her father's hatred of music. *Mother's love for Daddy had to be much greater than her love for her music.*

As a little girl, Nicole loved their visits to Aunt Kathryn's. The white baby grand piano stood in the parlor of her Victorian home. At the age of four when her family visited Aunt Kathryn, she would pick out the simple songs that she had intently listened to on her Playschool and Fisher Price toys. Her father would leave the room in disgust at the sound of his small daughter's passion for playing the piano.

With the grace of an eagle, the plane touched down on the runway. "Maybe I'll see you around," Kevin said as he gathered his things from the overhead compartment.

Ha, she thought, *Pittsburgh is a big city, fat chance our paths will cross.*

Aunt Kathryn's smiling face and open arms welcome Nicole as she entered the terminal. The unspoken joy of being together resonated between them.

Nicole's nonstop chatter about the Children's Music Forum amused Kathryn. *If only my brother could accept her enthusiasm and talent.* She thought.

They collected Nicole's luggage. The anticipation of being able to spend hours playing the piano at Aunt Kathryn's house was so exciting. It would be a wonderful replacement for the few hours of practice in the school music lab while she waited for her brother to finish his sports practices. Yet the reality that it would only last for a few weeks made her sad. She had set her sights on participating in the Children's Music Forum and nothing was going to stand in the way of her doing her best. The possibility of meeting the famous Madam Maxine was a dream come true.

Nicole loved Pittsburgh. The mid-morning flight allowed time for lunch and some site seeing around the city. There was something mysterious and enchanting about Pittsburgh. They rode the incline to the top of Mount Washington, Nicole's favorite spot, overlooking, The Point, where the Allegheny and the Monongahela rivers come together to form the Ohio river. Thus, sometimes called Three Rivers, Heinz Field, the football stadium, and PNC Park the baseball stadium.

The warm sun and gentle breeze made for a pleasant walk around the fountain at Point State park.

Nicole's excitement to get her hands on the piano made the short drive from the city to Aunt Kathryn's house seem extra-long.

CHAPTER 3

"I know your first order of business will be to get your hands on the piano keys," Kathryn chuckled as they pulled into the garage. "We will unpack your things and get you settled into your room later."

Nicole and Devin had always had their own rooms at Aunt Kathryn's house.

"I love it," Nicole, squealed with delight as she placed her luggage in her room. A portrait of Madam Maxine hung above the bed, accented with large music notes. *Aunt Kathryn understands my love for music and that Madam Maxine is my idol.* She thought laying her purse on the bed.

She ran to the kitchen, where Aunt Kathryn was preparing them a snack. Lemon aide and fresh fruit was so refreshing for a warm afternoon. "I love my room, thank you so much for the lovely portrait of Madam Maxine." Nicole said wrapping her arms around Kathryn's waist.

"I'm looking forward to hearing you play some of the music you have been working on." Kathryn said.

"I just hope I can play good enough to make Madam Maxine proud of me."

"As long as you do your very best that is all that can be expected."

"I have a whole week to practice as many hours a day as I want now that I'm here and have a piano, practicing a few hours a week after school in the music lab, just wasn't enough."

"What have you chosen for your presentation?" Kathryn asked.

"I had three selections, Chopin's Nocturne, Beethoven's Fur Elise, and an arrangement of Ave Maria, but I've chosen Chopin's Nocturne."

"All three of those are a bit complicated for a beginner," Kathryn answered.

"I chose Chopin's Nocturne, I've listened to the Madam Maxine CD you gave me so much, I hope that someday I can play it just like she does."

Kathryn followed Nicole into the parlor where the white baby grand piano stood waiting for someone to bring its keys to life. "With my busy work schedule, I don't have much time to play the piano anymore." Kathryn said.

The piano rang clear as a water fall as Nicole put her fingers to the keys.

"That was beautiful," Kathryn said, with a glint of pride in her eyes, when Nicole struck the last note. "You have always found a way to accomplish anything that was important to you."

"But I could be so much better if I had my own piano. Daddy buys me expensive gifts and gives me almost anything I want but he refuses to let me have a piano. Do you know why he hates music so much?" Nicole asked.

"That is something I could never figure out. When you were about four or five years old the first thing you would do when your family came to visit me was go to the piano, it amazed me that you could pick out songs that you had listen to on your musical toys. Your Father would always leave the room. I never knew why."

"Mother must not have known about his hatred for music before she married him," Nicole replied.

"Or her love for him was greater than her love for her music" Kathryn answered.

Nicole continued to dreamily play every song that flowed through her mind.

THE PIANO

"I have arranged my schedule so that we will have time to visit some of the attractions around the city this week." Kathryn said.

"I will be happy just being here with you and playing the piano all day long." Nicole answered.

"There are several summer music programs at the Mary Pappert School of Music at Duquesne University. I thought you might enjoy attending some of them."

I would like to see Heinz Hall. Isn't that where many of the concerts in Pittsburgh are held?"

"I have season tickets to the symphony they will be performing there on Wednesday night. I thought you would like to go. For now, it is time to say good-night."

Nicole could hardly control her excitement. She found it hard to fall asleep.

When she opened her eyes the next morning, she thought *no it's not a dream I'm really here and the piano is waiting for me.*

Aunt Kathryn was already in the kitchen making breakfast.

"I have a few morning appointments then I'm free this afternoon for us to explore the city." She said when Nicole entered the kitchen. "Today would be a beautiful day to visit the Phipps Conservatory and Botanical Gardens, the spring flowers are so beautiful now and I think you will enjoy the Butterfly Forest."

Nicole hurriedly finished her breakfast. She could not waste a minute of practice time.

"I will be finished with my appointments by two," Kathryn said. Kissing Nicole goodbye.

I know it's just the music Daddy rejects, but why? These thoughts always made her want to cry. She banged the piano keys getting louder and louder with each octave this was her way of releasing her frustration. Then she quietly flowed into, Ave Maria. the melody that sooth her feelings of anger and calmed her spirit.

Aunt Kathryn's encouragement to not give up on her natural talent was her lifeline.

Ignoring Aunt Kathryn's suggestion of choosing a more simplistic arrangement or an easier selection of music, Nicole continued to practice for several hours, her heart was set on playing Chopin's Nocturne to perfection.

"That was beautiful," Aunt Kathryn said.

Nicole was so engrossed in her music that she was startled by Aunt Kathryn voice. "Have you taken a break for lunch?"

"I lost all track of time."

"I'm sorry, my appointments ran a little longer than I expected and the traffic out of the city was horrendous today."

"That's okay, you need to rest." Nicole said. "I will make us some lunch I was just lost in my practice."

"You cannot let your music isolate you from the world."

"We will have plenty of time to go site seeing after the performance is over."

"Tomorrow my schedule is clear, we can go to the Phipps Conservatory and Botanical Gardens then, it would give us the whole day to leisurely enjoy the beauty of the gardens."

Last night's rain brought a freshness to the dawn of a new day, the sun glistened on the rain drops across the lawn. Aunt Kathryn was relaxing on the porch with her morning coffee. Nicole loved having breakfast on the porch with Aunt Kathryn. "I can't believe I slept so late," Nicole said, pouring herself a glass of juice.

"It's only eight o'clock." Kathryn answered.

"Do I have time to practice before we go?"

"Just don't get so lost in your music that you forget to eat sleep and breath," Kathryn chuckled.

"I have never seen so many different kinds of butterflies!" Nicole exclaimed as they entered the Butterfly Forest.

"Dr Yaffa!"

THE PIANO

"Louise, I haven't seen you in ages."

"Kevin!" Nicole exclaimed. Turning to greet Aunt Kathryn's friend.

"You two know each other?" Aunt Kathryn questioned, surprised.

"We met on the plane. Nicole replied.

"This is my grandson," Louise said. "He is playing in the annual soccer tournament to benefit the Children's Hospital Cancer Center; he will be spending a couple of weeks with me."

"Nicole is my niece; she is spending the summer with me."

"We will be playing our first game tomorrow afternoon," Kevin said turning to Nicole. "Would you like to come and watch? It's for a good cause."

Not wanting to be rude, Nicole Answered, "I'm participating in the Children's Music Forum on Saturday and I must practice." The excuse I must practice had become her way out of anything she didn't want to do.

"I'm not really into music, Kevin replied, but…I'll Make a deal with you, if you come to my game I'll come to your performance."

The strange way they met and running into each other in a city as big as Pittsburgh made Nicole think there could be a friendship different from the kids in her school. Kevin had a purpose in his life. "Deal." She said reaching to shake his hand.

"A soccer game might be fun," Aunt Kathryn said as they drove home, "I've never had the chance to see Devin play."

"I'm not so sure of that," Nicole answered, "but a deal is a deal."

After dinner Nicole spent several hours practicing, she could feel the improvement in the music but was still not satisfied, there was just something not right yet. Aunt Kathryn joined her at the piano, and they played a crazy little duet.

"You make me want to get back to playing again." Kathryn said. "Sometimes we let our life get so busy we forget to stop and enjoy the things in life that gives us pleasure."

"That was fun playing a duet with you." Nicole said,

"It was, I have an early morning appointment. It's time to say goodnight."

"How long does it take to get to the soccer field?" Nicole asked finishing her breakfast.

"About forty-five minutes, you have time for a couple hours of practice. I would have rescheduled this appointment, but this little girl just finished her chemo treatments last week, I'm hoping to release her with a clean bill of health today."

"I hope so too," Nicole replied. "I'm glad Kevin is supporting such a good cause."

Dreading an hour and a half of watching a soccer game instead of being at the piano working on her music, Nicole reluctantly honored the deal she had made with Kevin.

This event drew a large crowd. "The fund raisers for Children's Hospital always has great support." Kathryn said as they were able to secure seats at the middle of the field. "They will be playing at both ends of the field and we will be able to see them from here." Nicole answered.

"Go Kevin!" Nicole shouted as Kevin approached the net for a goal. She couldn't believe she was cheering at a soccer game. "Way to go Kevin!" she shouted as he scored his third goal.

"I wish Devin was here." Nicole said as they returned to the car. *Why is this game so different from watching my brother play?* She wondered.

"You seemed to enjoy the game," Aunt Kathryn said.

"I did," Nicole replied. "Maybe I created a dislike for the game because I focused too much on Daddy's interest for Devin and his sports but will never give a second look at what I would like to do. Is that jealously?"

"It's natural for you to want your parent's approval of what you do and have them be proud of you."

THE PIANO

"I let the bullying at school make me more determined than ever to accomplish my dream even if I don't have the instrument, I need to become a professional."

"Your natural music talent and determination will help you rise above those setbacks."

"I haven't made any friends at my new school. Do you think my constant obsession with my music and no interest in sports has clouded my relationship with other students?"

"I believe your music has kept you from falling into discouragement and depression that sometimes leads many young people to fall into the trap of suicide because of the bulling they experience at school."

"I've never thought about suicide but sometimes I wish I were back at my old school. Public school was supposed to be much more fun than private school."

"Have you talked to your parents about this?"

"I don't think they would understand."

"Just because your father doesn't agree about your music doesn't mean he would not understand your desire to be in a better school."

"Aunt Kathryn, you always help shine a different light on things."

"When your parents come back from their trip I will speak to your father about his dislike for music. Maybe he will open up to me about what causes his strong objection to you having a piano."

"Thank you." Nicole said hugging Aunt Kathryn.

"I think it's time for a snack and then good-night. Tomorrow will be a good day for a shopping trip."

"When do you think Madam Maxine will be coming to Pittsburgh?"

"I would think it will be in the next few days. She probably has a lot of preparation to get ready for the Children's Music Forum on Saturday."

CHAPTER 4

Madam Maxine had played her last performance on the New York stages three weeks ago. In spite of a life full of practices and performances; she had managed to find time to work with the Children's Music Forum she had founded, to help gifted children develop their music talent. This filled the void she carried inside of her from the loss of her own children. In just a little over a month she would be hosting the first Children's Music Forum in Pittsburgh. Maxine had sponsored many programs over the years, but this was the first time in her hometown.

Over the years some of her participants had earned scholarships to the Juilliard School of Music here in the city, it blessed her heart to know that she had played an important role in a student's life that set them on the path to a successful music career.

Retirement sounds so boring after 30 years on stage, she thought.

I am closing my New York apartment and opening a new chapter in my life. Twenty-five years of memories were about to be packed in boxes. Some would go to the new apartment in Pittsburgh, Pennsylvania, others to Goodwill and the rest would end up in storage until she was settled somewhere permanent.

Maxine felt an arrow of anxiety shoot through her heart. In the midst of all the boxes, and the decisions she was faced with, she began to reflect on her music career and what had brought her to this point in her life.

THE PIANO

The piano that had been so much a part of her life, now stood before her like a colossal mountain. It had claimed one whole room of her small New York apartment for the past twenty-five years. Now Maxine was faced with a decision she thought she would never have to make. *What will be the fate of the one piece of my life that has brought me through so much, both joy and sorrow, heartache, and livelihood. It had been my comfort and my voice, my life.* "NOW WHAT!" She exclaimed.

The piano was a constant reminder of her foolishness, as a young aspiring pianist, to let a man in a military uniform draw her into an impulsive relationship that not only stifled her music career but turned her life into a disaster.

The night before Frank's return from his last tour of duty in Viet Nam, played in her head like a re-run of an old movie.

She had embraced his return with mixed emotions. *I should have been ecstatic that he was returning, many of his comrades were not so lucky.*

After eighteen months of single parenting and working a full-time job Maxine was drained. The stress of raising the children alone and giving up her music made her angry and resentful.

"What will this new chapter of retirement, bring into my life?" She questioned. "You and I must part company." She said starring at the piano. *How can I just let go of the one thing that has molded and shaped my life for so many years?* Maxine placed her hands on the piano keys. "Your music was like pristine water to my parched and thirsty soul. You brought life to me in my time of sorrow and carried me through many rough years."

Every Christmas from the time she was six years Maxine would ask Santa for a black ebony baby grand piano.

At the age of eight she had begun taking piano lessons from her grade school music teacher, practicing on her Grandmother's old upright piano. Along the way she had several teachers, they all told her parents that her natural music ability needed to be cultivated, it would be a sin not to develop that talent.

After graduation from high school, Maxine's parents spent thousands of dollars for her to attend the Carnegie Mellon School of Music and bought the black ebony baby grand piano that she had dreamed of for so many years.

Maxine's music professor had received a request for a student to auditioned for a backup pianist for the Pittsburgh Symphony at Heinz Hall. He recommended Maxine. She was accepted for the position.

Just being in the presence of so many talented musicians caused her to set her sights on bigger and better things. Someday she would take her place on the big stage.

While attending the Carnegie Mellon School of Music Maxine played at night clubs and special events. It was at one of those special events that Frank, a career army officer, his tall lean stature, that uniform and his smooth talk had swept Maxine off her feet. After a short whirlwind courtship, they were married.

Maxime tried to put her thoughts to rest. *Returning to the place of all my painful memories may not be the wisest decision I've made in my life.* She thought.

For twenty-five years, through tears and a broken heart she performed on Broadway and other New York City stages, now she was putting all of that aside, and returning to the place where her dream began and quickly turned into a nightmare.

Maxine had returned many times to search for her children. Each time she got a tip as to where they were their father had taken them somewhere else.

She sent cards and letters to his Post Office box and had never received any reply, then one day her agent received a package addressed to her with no return address. It contained all the unopened cards and letters she had sent to the children over the years with a note. 'Do not send any more cards, to us you are dead.'

Maxine pulled her attention back to the task of sorting and packing. She took the four boxes from the closet shelf with each of

THE PIANO

her children's names on them. John, Luke, Ben, and Kathryn. The sadness that had plagued her for the past twenty-five years, began to rise- up in her. These treasurer boxes contained all the cards and letters that were returned to her, each year she had added birthday and holiday cards in the hopes that someday she would see her children again. *Maybe, just maybe, once I'm back in Pittsburgh there will be a trace of them. What have they done with their lives? Did they marry? Do they have families of their own? Do I have grandchildren somewhere? Were they successful? Did the boys follow in their father's footsteps and join the military?*

"No, no I can't dwell on those things, there is still much packing to do and many decisions to make." She cautioned herself.

After a restless night and very-little sleep Maxine faced the day with much apprehension. Questioning her decision to return to her hometown, she poured another cup of coffee. *The only person I've kept in touch with is my high school friend Margert, I haven't seen her since she came to visit me more than ten years ago. Once I get settled, I will contact her, maybe we can catch up for old time sake.*

The movers arrived promptly at nine. Maxine took command, giving them the address of her new apartment, directing them as to what was to go there. "The piano will go into storage at your company's headquarters in Pittsburgh." She informed the driver.

"And what are we supposed to do with all that is left?" He asked.

"The apartment complex manager is going to take care of that."

Maxine gathered her luggage, called a taxi, and headed to the airport.

The flight from New York City to Pittsburgh was uneventful. Maxine entered the baggage claim area, still questioning her decision to return to her hometown.

"Maxine, where have you been for the past twenty-five years?"

That voice, I know that voice, she thought.

Turning slowly, she came face to face with a tall white-haired gentleman. "Mr. Roberts!" She exclaimed. "How did you recognize me after all these years?"

"You were one of my best students at the Carnegie Mellon School of Music." He said, staring at her as if he couldn't believe it was really her. "After you graduated, I followed your performances here in the city until they abruptly came to an end. May I have the pleasure of your company over a cup of coffee?" He asked.

Seated at a small table in the corner of the coffee shop, Maxine sipped her coffee. "Did you continue your music career?" Mr. Roberts asked.

"I've played on many New York City stages."

"Will you be performing here in Pittsburgh again?"

"I'm retired." She replied. *I can't just unload the whole ugly story of my life on him.*

"What brings your back to your hometown?"

"I will be conducting a Children's Music Forum at Mt. Lebanon Senior High School."

"You are the famous Madam Maxine!" He asked, surprised. "I saw the ads for the program, but I never connected Madam Maxine with my student Maxine"

"That's me," she answered just a little embarrassed.

"Well, I'll be…it blesses me to know that I played a part in sending one of my students to the big stage. And no one deserved it more than you."

"Will you be my guest at the Children's Music Forum?"

"Will you be playing?"

"No, young musicians become intimidated when a professional performs before their presentation. I don't want to make the young participants nervous; it would affect their performance."

"May I request a private concert?"

THE PIANO

"Once the Children's Music Forum is over possibly, we could get together again for coffee." She answered, handing him her phone number.

"Or dinner." He replied smiling. "Will you be staying in town for a while?"

"I've rented an apartment in Greentree."

"You're moving here?"

"At least temporarily,"

Mr. Roberts sensed that Maxine didn't want to reveal her plans, so he didn't pursue the matter any further.

"May I drive you to your apartment?"

"Where you waiting for someone to arrive?"

"I have just returned from visiting my son in New Mexico."

Grateful that she didn't have to fight the line at the rent-a-car desk Maxine gladly accept Mr. Roberts offer.

Maxine marveled at the changes of the landscape along the Parkway from the airport to Greentree. "Everything has changed so much since I've been gone."

"It has been twenty-five years; progress doesn't stand still." Mr. Roberts replied.

"The airport was almost frightening; it has expanded so much."

"The city has undergone many changes, most of them for the better. The steel mills are gone."

"That's a good thing, the air must be cleaner and more breathable."

"Many of the old bridges with stone support pillars have been replaced with safer steel structures."

"Some people used to call Pittsburgh the city of bridges."

"Now it could be called the city of hospitals and education." Mr. Roberts replied. "The campuses of the University of Pittsburgh and Carnegie Mellon have expanded significantly, and the hospitals just keep adding new facilities."

"I guess I have a lot of catching up to do."

"There have been numerous landmarks constructed."

"What about the old Heidelberg racetrack? My father loved to go there, but my mother would never go with him, she hated the noise and dust."

"It's gone the Raceway Plaza now occupies that parcel of land."

"What about Heinz Hall and the Heinz Plant on the North Side?"

"Heinz Hall is still hosting music concerts and programs. The Heinz plant is now the H J Heinz museum."

"I never thought they would stop making Heinz ketchup."

"Best ketchup in the world. They still make it just not here in Pittsburgh."

"I remember when Heinz introduced a new product, they gave donations to non-profit groups who would come and do taste tests."

"When you get settled in, I would like to show you around, take in a concert at Heinz Hall, maybe ride the incline to the top of Mt Washington for dinner." Mr. Roberts said as he opened the car door for her.

"I would like that."

Amused Maxine thought, *at his age he is still young at heart. I did sort of have a crush on him when he was my professor.*

Maxine entered the apartment complex manager's office and request the key to her new apartment.

"Your apartment coordinator took care of all the necessary details with the movers." The manager said handing Maxine her key.

She entered the foyer. *I left an apartment full of packed boxes now I'm standing in the middle of a mountain of boxes to be unpacked.* She thought. *Is there even a remote chance that I will locate my children. If I do would they want to open their hearts and accept me after all these years?*

CHAPTER 5

Nicole poured herself a glass of juice and joined Aunt Kathryn on the porch where she was enjoying her morning coffee with breakfast waiting for Nicole.

The anticipation of a shopping trip with Aunt Kathryn was overshadowed by the realization that the Children's Music Forum was only four days away.

How does Madam Maxine dress when she performs on stage? Nicole wondered.

"Are you ready for a day of girl time and shopping?" Aunt Kathryn asked.

"As much as I love shopping and spending time with you… the Children's Music Forum is only four days away and I want my presentation to be perfect."

"I listened to Madam Maxine's CD last night and I think your rendition of Chopin's Nocturne is sounding much like the way she plays it."

"I want it to be perfect."

"The only way for it to be perfect is for you to inject your own style and passion into it. You must feel the pattern of the music and play it with that passion. You must develop your own style and deliver it to the listener with great expression and meaning. That is how you become a great musician."

Nicole pondered Aunt Kathryn's words. "I just feel so inadequate because I haven't had any formal music lessons. I'm sure the other participants have probably had several years of lessons."

"Those who have a natural ability to play by ear often put much more feeling and expression into the music they play."

Aunt Kathryn's advice always helped Nicole to look at things in a different way. "If I practice for an hour this morning, then take a break, I may have a fresh approach to the music."

"My Friend, Louise, invited us to have dinner with her and her grandson Kevin on the Gateway Clipper tonight."

"Kevin seems like a nice guy, but I need to focus on my music for the performance."

"You can't let the obsession with your music shut out the whole world."

Is it an obsession or is it a shield that keeps me from feeling the sting of rejection? Nicole silently questioned. *Or is it my line of defense to keep me from becoming involved in the reckless actions of my classmates?*

"I guess you're right, a shopping trip will help me focus my attention on something else for a little while. How do you think Madame Maxime dresses for her performances?"

"Sweetie, this is about you, your style of dress, your style of music, it's about you."

Nicole finished her breakfast and went into the parlor, the piano stood waiting to speak whatever language and tone Nicole's fingers released on the keys.

"I have a couple of errands to run this morning while you practice, then we will grab a quick lunch in the Food Court at the mall before we shop." Aunt Kathryn said. "We will meet Louise and Kevin at Station Square at six, the cruise boards at six-fifteen.

Maybe my music would flow better if I am more relaxed, Nicole thought as she let her fingers flow up and down the keyboard in no particular rhythm.

THE PIANO

Nicole was so lost in her music that when Aunt Kathryn returned it seemed she had only been gone a shot time, not more than an hour.

"If we arrive at Station Square early, we will be able to go to the Bessemer Court and see the Waltzing Water Fountain with its Liquid Fireworks Show of hundreds of multi- colored water jets all choreographed to music. They soar up to forty feet in the air. They also have many nice shops there." Aunt Kathryn said entering the parlor where Nicole was absorbed in her music.

"That sounds like more fun than going to the mall." Nicole answered.

"There are so many beautiful things to see and do around the city. After the Children's Music forum is over, we will explore more of them."

Nicole was in awe of the beauty of the Grand Concourse. "This structure, built in 1898, housed the terminal of the Pittsburg and Lake Eire Railroad and many trains of the Baltimore and Ohio Railroad past through here." Nicole read from the plaque on the wall.

They entered the Grand Concourse restaurant. "This is such a beautiful place!" Nicole exclaimed.

"It is wonderful that the Pittsburgh Historical and Landmark Foundation has preserved the history and beauty of this place."

"That was such a delicious lunch. I'm so glad I decided to give my music a rest and come here with you."

"It's time to do some shopping."

There was such a variety of shops, "This certainly is different than shopping at the mall." Nicole said as they entered the Nautical shop. "That outfit would be perfect for our boat trip on the river!" She exclaimed pointing to the navy-blue shirt with a white anchor on the sleeve and the white skirt with a navy- blue anchor on the front of it. "I guess I can't wear it tonight there is nowhere to change."

"I know the woman at the register, I will ask her if after I pay for it, can you change in the dressing room?"

Looking like a real shipmate Nicole proudly modeled her new outfit.

"We have one more stop before we meet Louise and Kevin, The Bessemer Court to see the Waltzing Water Fountain." Aunt Kathryn said.

"Thank you for such a beautiful day." Nicole said as she took in the breath-taking beauty of the Waltzing Water Fountain and its liquid fireworks.

"We are not finished yet. The Sunset and Dinner Cruise has much more beauty to offer.

"Ship Ahoy," Kevin said, giving Nicole a high five, as she and Aunt Kathryn approached the bench where he and his grandmother were sitting. "You look like you are ready to sail."

Kevin waited until Nicole, Kathryn and his grandmother had boarded the Gateway Clipper. He held each of the women's chairs as they were seated at their table.

Other than her father Nicole had never had a boy hold her chair for her to be seated. *He is so different from the boys at my school.*

Seated at a table with a view of the Pittsburgh skyline, Kathryn and Louise began to catch-up on what had taken place in their lives since they had last seen each other.

The Gateway Clipper pulled away from the dock. The Captain welcomed the guests and invited them to enjoy their dinner. "We will be cruising on the Monongahela, Allegheny and Ohio rivers. We will go thru the Emsworth Locks and Dam, on the Ohio River, this will give you a slight idea of how the Panama Canal works."

"Do you visit your Grandmother often?" Nicole asked.

"Not as often as I would like to, school and my soccer club keeps me pretty busy, my soccer club travels in the summer."

"My brother plays soccer and runs track; he plays in a year-round soccer league, but they only travel for tournaments."

"I'm sure your music keeps you busy."

THE PIANO

Nicole withdrew into her world of silence not wanting to share the ugly details of her struggles to accomplish her dream of becoming a concert pianist.

This is so strange, I'm really enjoying Kevin's friendship, Nicole thought as he led the way to the top deck.

She turned her face to the clear cloudless sky. Kevin smiled, remembering their encounter at the airport, as he brushed a lock of hair from her forehead. "There is so much to see and do in Pittsburgh. We could do some sight- seeing." He said.

"I can't," *but I want to,* she thought. "I can't until after the Children's Music Forum is over."

"After that we will have some time."

"I would like that."

The Pittsburgh skyline, with the backdrop of a beautiful sunset was a magnificent sight. Kevin detected her reluctance to talk about herself and her music, he changed the subject. "Do you come to Pittsburgh often?" He asked.

"We visit my Aunt Kathryn a couple times a year. This is the first I've come for the summer. My mother accompanied my father on a trip overseas to take care of some important business."

"They are gone for the whole summer, what about your brother?"

"He's at the lake with our cousins and then he will go to soccer camp."

The boat entered the locks, the water rose lifting it up for the water level to be the same height as the water they would exit into.

"That was really exciting. I've never done anything like that before." Nicole said.

"It's been a long time since I have," Kevin replied. "When I was little my grandfather would bring me here."

That faraway look in his eyes cautioned Nicole to be silent for a moment as Kevin relived those special times with his grandfather.

Aunt Kathryn and Louise were still chatting when Kevin and Nicole returned to their table.

The Gateway Clipper docked, "Thank you all for joining us this evening," the Captain said. "Have a wonderful visit to our great city of Pittsburgh."

"Thank you for such a lovely evening" Kathryn said hugging Louise. "It was fun catching up on old times."

"See you on Saturday," Kevin said, giving Nicole a fist bump.

"Never in my wildest dreams," Nicole left her sentence dangle in mid-air.

"Never in your wildest dreams what?" Aunt Kathryn asked unlocking the car door.

"When we got off the plane Kevin said maybe I'll see you around. In a city the size of Pittsburgh who would have thought we had a chance of running into each other."

"That was quite a coincidence. I hadn't seen Louise in such a long time, I didn't know much about her family. You and Kevin seemed to have a nice time."

"Kevin is so different from the boys at my school, he is so much more mature and polite. I did have a nice time talking to him. A friend like him may give me a different outlook on joining in some other activities. My music is an escape from all the nonsense that goes on around me at school."

"He came on the plane from Charlotte with you, do you know what school he goes to there?"

"I'm not sure he is from, Charlotte, he said his Soccer club travels in the summer he may have just been traveling from one of his team's games."

"I'm glad he's coming to your performance on Saturday."

"Me too."

"This has been such a lovely day. I'm glad you took a break from your music and had such a wonderful time."

THE PIANO

"However, the next three days I will have to do some intense practice."

"Tomorrow evening is the symphony at Heinz Hall."

Ready for a good night's sleep Nicole hugged Aunt Kathryn. "Thank you for such a wonderful day, good-night."

Aunt Kathryn had already gone to work when Nicole woke up. She read the note on the kitchen table. I'm not sure how my day will go. If I have no emergencies, I should be finished by three. There is plenty of food in the fridge. If you need me just call my cell. The symphony is at seven o'clock.

Nicole poured a glass of juice, grabbed a couple of pop tarts, and put on her headphones, to listen to Chopin's Nocturne on Madam Maxine's CD before she began her practice. *A whole day of just me and the piano.*

Kathryn returned home to find Nicole pretending she was on the big stage as she practiced her music.

"I have secured a backstage pass for after tonight's performance."

"How did you do that?"

Nicole questioned surprised.

"Being a pediatrician, I have taken care of many of these musician's children, one of them was a patient today. When I spoke to his mother of how much music means to you, she gave me a pass to meet the musicians after the performance tonight."

What could be more exciting than being surrounded by a room full of musicians and their conductor. Nicole thought, as they entered the auditorium.

She stood in awe of the beauty of Heinz Hall.

"Madam Maxine played here, maybe someday I will too."

CHAPTER 6

Nicole and Aunt Kathryn entered the auditorium. Nicole took her place with the other contestants, seated in alphabetical order. This meant Nicole would be the last performer. Aunt Kathryn and the other parents were seated across the aisle from the contestants.

With a million butterflies floating in her stomach Nicole hoped these last two days of intense practice would help her perform Chopin's Nocturne in a way that would impress Madam Maxine. Her bright yellow dress highlighted the sparkle of excitement and anticipation in her chocolate brown eyes.

Madame Maxine's appearance and gentle manner took Nicole's breath away. She shook her head as if waking from a dream. *I'm really here in the same room with Madam Maxine.*

Madam Maxine stepped to the microphone. "I am happy to welcome all of our participants and guess to the First Children's Music Forum in Pittsburgh. The Children's Music Form is an organization that encourages young musicians to develop their music talent, it also provides scholarships to outstanding young musicians. We have awarded scholarships to outstanding students who have attended the Juilliard School of Music in New York City, one of the top music schools in the country." Madam Maxine paused and turned to address the children, "I'm honored to be planting the seed of music into your lives. Your participation today is for you to express the sheer pleasure of your talent and desire to become an accomplished musician."

She turned back to the audience, "I want to thank you all for coming this afternoon and my charge to you parents, friends and relatives of these young musicians is to encourage and support them as they continue to develop their talents, in their quest for a future career in music."

I wish my parents were here, oh if Daddy could only understand how much this means to me.

Madam Maxine's soft voice set Nicole's mind at ease.

"All of our judges for today's performance are accomplished musicians who have performed on stages across the country and around the world in many different levels of musical productions.

She turned to address the children again. "The real you is the person you are now with all your imperfections but to become the person you dream of being, you must have confidence in yourself, accept yourself, embrace your creativity, believe in yourself, and take it one step at a time. Overcome your fears, fear destroys more dreams then failure. Never let something impact your life to the point that it destroys your confidence and your happiness."

Listening to Madam Maxine's encouraging words inspired Nicole to continue her love for the piano even though the only practice time she had was a few hours a week in the school's music lab. *I would have no practice time during this summer if I wasn't here with Aunt Kathryn.*

Madam Maxine continued to admonish the children. "Becoming a professional musician requires talent, desire and commitment. Education is your passport to the future, but your determination is the fuel you need to make that journey. Find the real you through your music. When you feel the pattern of the music, you can produce it with great expression and meaning to the listener."

Those are the words Aunt Kathryn spoke to me the other day. Nicole thought.

"Music is like poetry; both are made up of similar phrases. A musical phrase is made up of a certain number of tones grouped in a melodic pattern. A poetic phrase is made up of a group of words in the form to fit the type of poetry being expressed."

Nicole was so engrossed in what Madam Maxine was saying she did not notice Kevin slip into the seat next to Aunt Kathryn.

"This poem, I do not know the author, but it is such an expression of what music is.

Music speaks what cannot be expressed.
Sooths the mind and gives it rest.
Heals the heart and makes it whole.
Flows from heaven to the soul."

Maxine turned her attention to the group of young musicians. "Now I have the pleasure of introducing our honored guests and performers.

"Please, Lord don't let anyone else be playing Chopin's Nocturne," Nicole whispered.

As each performer was announced they took their place at the piano and performed their selection of music.

Abby Beckley, will be performing James Bastien's arrangement of "Surprise Symphony."

"David Costa's selection is, J.S Bach's "Minute in G major."

"Casey Kirk, has selected Franz Joseph Hayden's Minute in G."

Donald Mason will be giving his rendition of Ludwig van Beethoven's Russian Folk Song".

"Kylie Wilson, has selected Franz Schubert's Waltz C."

Nicole sat on the edge of her seat waiting for her name to be announced.

They all are so accomplished in their music. I hope my presentation is comparable to their performances.

Madam Maxine listened intently as each contestant gave their presentation.

"Our last contestant for the afternoon is Nicole Ya…Yaffa." Maxine's heart leaped in her chest. *That is an exceedingly rare name,*

THE PIANO

this is the city where my children disappeared. Could she be…no, no, don't let your imagination runaway with you.

"Nicole Yaffa will now perform Chopin's Nocturne."

Nicole was a slender, small breasted girl, with an erect carriage which she accented by throwing her body backwards at the shoulders like a young cadet as she approached the piano.

Nicole approached the piano with a reverence for the instrument and took command of the keyboard with a confidence beyond that of any of the other contestants. For a moment, her fingers hovered over the keys, as she lowered them the piano awakened like clear freshwater bubbling over the rocks in a stream. Her long fingers glided over the keys and the music flowed like an eagle soaring through the air. As the notes rose from the piano keys, Nicole's heart rose with them.

Nicole struck the last note, Madam Maxine marveled at the young woman's performance, the excellent tempo, the flow, and expression of the music was performed to perfection. Her dynamics and technique were flawless.

Her interpretation was much like I would play it myself. Maxine thought. *This child's love for her music reminds me of my own love of music when I was young.*

Maxine could not dismiss the similarity of Nicole's features, her eyes that sparkled like chocolate diamonds, the long lashes, the olive complexion, and her wavy black hair are so like the traits of the Yaffa family. Those long slender fingers are perfect for a pianist. "Lord have I returned to my hometown to find the family that was taken away from me all those years ago?" She questioned.

Mesmerized by such a performance of Chopin's Nocturne, by a young musician, Madam Maxine waited for the judge's decision.

Gaining control of her emotions, Madam Maxine returned to the stage and presented certificates of appreciation to the participants for their performance.

The judge handed Maxine the envelope containing their final decision.

With a lump in her throat, and choking back tears she announced, "The trophy for the top performance today goes to Nicole Yaffa for her rendition of Chopin's Nocturne." The excitement shot through Nicole's body like a bolt of lightning, tears streamed down her face. Approaching the front of the stage she thought her legs were going to fold under her.

With one hand holding the trophy, Madam Maxine, hugged Nicole with the other one. "A musician's natural ability to play speaks through the music they play. Nicole accept your natural ability to play the piano. It is a gift. Natural ability teamed with lessons and much practice makes a great pianist.

My dream was to meet her she actually hugged me. The only way I will be able to improve my music is practice, practice. Nicole thought, still in a daze from all that had taken place in the last few minutes.

Kevin raced to meet Nicole as she came down from the stage colliding with her a second time, this time instead of retrieving sheets of music he threw his arms around her neck, "you were absolutely amazing!"

Madam Maxine's anxiety mounted as she approached Nicole and Kathryn. "This is my Aunt Kathryn."

Kathryn displayed the same Yaffa traits as Nicole. *Kathryn is my daughter's name or was if her father didn't change it.* Maxine thought.

"Kathryn," Madam Maxine said extending her hand, wanting to grab Kathryn up in her arms.

"Part of the prize for the top contestant is to have dinner with me." Madam Maxine said. "We can arrange a day and time that is good for you."

This can't really be happening, Nicole thought. *My dream was to meet her, not only have I met her she hugged me and now she is inviting me to have dinner with her. This is more than a dream come true. If I'm dreaming, please don't wake me up.*

THE PIANO

Nicole was jolted back to reality by Aunt Kathryn's voice. "Tuesday evening would be wonderful."

"I must shake the hand of this talented young pianist" The white-haired gentleman said reaching for Nicole' hand.

"Mr. Roberts is a retired music professor from the Carnegie Mellon School of Music." Madam Maxine introduced him.

"If you follow the path this lovely lady did with her music," Mr. Roberts said. Smiling at Madam Maxine. "You will accomplish great things."

Kathryn and Madam Maxine exchanged phone numbers. "See you on Tuesday." Kathryn said.

"Is that dinner offer still on the table?" Maxine asked. Turning to Mr. Roberts.

"Yes, Madam Maxine" Mr. Roberts teased. "Where shall we go?"

"I'm now retired, and I think it's time to drop the Madam. Once again, I'm just Maxine. Mount Washington was always one of my favorite places when I lived in the city."

The lights of the city brought a flood of memories that Maxine thought she had put to rest a long time ago. The old wounds seemed to break wide open. *Meeting Nicole and Kathryn shines a whole new light on my coming home.*

"Listening to Nicole's performance took me back to the classroom with you at the piano. Mr. Roberts said as they were seated at their table. Nicole Yaffa…is she related to you?"

"It's a very long story but I think I've found what I've been searching for."

Puzzled by her answer Mr. Roberts decided not to press her for an answer.

"Are you ok?" Aunt Kathryn asked. "You've been so quiet all the way home."

"I just wish mother and daddy could have been here to share this moment with me." Nicole answered wishfully. "I guess it doesn't matter daddy wouldn't have let me do this. I miss them so much."

"I had a message from your father, they will be back next week. He said there are some details that are going to take more time to get resolved. He will have to go back some time in the future. For now, he is going to arrange for Devin to meet them here and we all will have some time together."

"How will I tell him what I've done? I'm sure he will be angry with me."

"I promise you I will do my best to resolve this issue of music with your father. He must let you develop this wonderful talent that you have."

Holding her trophy close to her heart, Nicole reflected on the events of the past two weeks. *I can't believe it's only been two weeks. Being able to play the piano as many hours a day as I desired, making a friend who appreciates my interest in music, it was even fun watching him play soccer. When my family gets home, I will be more supportive of Devin's sports.* Meeting Madam Maxine was the ultimate highlight of it all. Having dinner with her on Tuesday night will be the icing on the cake. It will be like being on top of the world.

"I am so proud of you," Aunt Kathryn said. "Your hard work and determination have set you on the path to accomplishing your dream."

"I don't know how that will happen without a piano."

"We will work on resolving that issue when your parents return. We have had a day of such great accomplishments and excitement, it's time for a good night's rest."

"My heart is so full I don't know if I will be able to sleep." Nicole said placing the music trophy on the piano.

CHAPTER 7

Nicole sat crossed legged on her bed trying to comprehend all that had taken place in the past two weeks, her heart ached longing to have her family to celebrate with her, yet she feared that her father was going to be terribly upset when he learned the truth. *I didn't lie to him; I just never gave him the details of my reason for wanting to spend the summer with Aunt Kathryn. I guess maybe that was sort 0f a lie.*

"Nicole," Aunt Kathryn called from the kitchen, "Are you ok?"

"I'll be down in a minute." Nicole replied.

"I'm surprised that you aren't at the piano already."

"I miss Mommy and Daddy and Devin so much. I just wish we all could have celebrated my trophy like we celebrate Devin's soccer and track wins."

Oh, if we could only find the reason for my brother's opposition to music, Kathryn thought taking Nicole in her arms. *I will try and get to the root of this when he returns.* "You have the most exciting time of your life to look forward to tonight, dinner with Madam Maxine."

"It still doesn't seem real."

"Well it is, and my office is closed on Tuesdays, you and I have this whole day together. Is there something you would like to do?"

"With this rain it will have to be something indoors."

"A movie would work." Aunt Kathryn said, checking the theater listings.

"There's an eleven AM. one about a young girl who ran away from home and discovers her desire to be an adult isn't enough to get her through the perils of life on her own. It's a comedy."

"That sounds like me. I thought I was ready to travel by myself until I found my seat on the plane was already assigned to someone else."

"And because you are a mature young lady you didn't panic, and everything worked out. If we go to the eleven o'clock showing that will give us plenty of time to relax this afternoon before we meet Madam Maxine for dinner at six."

"I would like to see Kevin again," Nicole said wishfully.

"He seems like a nice young man."

"He's interested in improving his life and making other people's lives better. The kids at my school don't focus on anything but themselves and they only do enough to get by."

Kathryn thought about her school days she was never in a school long enough to make friends. It was hard being in a new school, sometimes more than one school in a year. When she was Nicole's age, she made a vow to herself. 'I will come out on top.' It was difficult, her father showed no interest in her schooling. In college she and her roommate became accountability partners. They decided that everything they did or said must add value to the life of every person they met, in turn adding value to their lives as they pursued their quest for success. They were each other's support team. That's what I will be for Nicole.

"When we reach beyond ourselves, we not only improve our own life, but we may help someone get a new prospective on what they are facing in life."

"Kevin did that for me. I was jealous of how daddy focused on Devin's sports but would not even acknowledge my love of music. I can still show my support for my brother, it was fun watching Kevin's team play soccer."

THE PIANO

"When we change our attitude about a situation we can see and appreciate what it means to the other person."

"I still wish I could share this special time with my family."

I will do my best to find the answer to that problem when your parents return. Now let's go see what that silly girl thought she could accomplish once she was on her own."

Aunt Kathryn always had a way of making everything look brighter. Nicole thought as they entered the movie theater.

The attendant handed Aunt Kathryn their tickets. "No movie is complete without popcorn." Nicole announced.

Nicole and Aunt Kathryn were still laughing when they returned to their car, at some of the predicaments that young girl got herself into just because she didn't want to obey her parent's rules. In the end she decided it was better to live by the rules and have someone that cared enough to keep her safe.

"That was pretty funny, but I don't think I'm ready to live on my own yet." Nicole chuckled.

"I don't think your parents are ready to even let you think about that. Their rules are for your protection and safety."

The avalanche of thoughts rolling around in Nicole's head as she dressed to meet Madam Maxine seemed to have no rhyme or reason. *How am I going to talk to Madam Maxine when I can't even make any sense of what I'm thinking? There is so much I want to ask her, but I don't even know where to start.*

Aunt Kathryn's voice interrupted her thoughts. "It's time to go."

With a quick last-minute glance in the full-length mirror, Nicole took in a deep breath and ran downstairs.

Madam Maxine requested a table by the window. The view of the city from the Monterey Bay restaurant a top Mt. Washington was glorious. The Point, PNC Park, Heinz Field, and all the lights of the city gave a festive atmosphere to this delightful evening.

Nicole nervously twisted the corners of her napkin. She had a million questions she wanted to ask Madam Maxine, but what do you say to such a famous person?

"Nicole your performance at the Children's Music Forum on Saturday was suburb." Madam Maxine said taking Nicole's hand.

Nicole was so nervous "Thank you," she replied barely above a whisper.

"How long have you been taking lessons?"

Nicole stared at her hands and continued to twist her napkin. "I don't really take lessons." She replied choking back tears.

"You don't!" Madam Maxine exclaimed.

For what seemed like forever Madam Maxine was silent. "I am amazed at your music talent. How have you become such an excellent pianist?"

"When my fingers touch the keys, whatever music is flowing through my mind just flows through my fingertips onto the piano keys. It's something I don't understand, but I love it so much.

"It is an amazing gift."

"I practice in the school music lab while I wait for my brother Devin to finish his sports practice."

"That is all the time you spend cultivating this wonderful talent?"

"My father is violently opposed to me becoming a concert pianist." Nicole blurred out. "He refuses to allow me to have a piano and take lessons. He would let me do anything as long as it doesn't involve music."

"For some reason my brother John, Nicole's father refuses to allow musical instruments in his house." Kathryn volunteered "From the time Nicole was a toddler she would pick out the tunes from her musical toys, on the piano when they visited me."

Maxine became quiet again. *John is one of my sons.* "Kathryn do you have any other siblings?"

THE PIANO

"I have two other brothers." Kathryn answered, wondering why Madam Maxine was so interested in her family. "Ben went into the army right out of High School, when he came home, he was so withdrawn, he doesn't have much interaction with us. Luke is an Air Force Pilot.

Ben and Luke, Maxine fought back her tears. "I asked you to have dinner with me tonight for two reasons. First it was part of the prize for the winner of the Children's Music Forum, I can't believe this young lady, who has never taken lessons gave such an excellent rendition of Chopin's Nocturne. Secondly, I was so impressed with Nicole's performance that I want to encourage her to cultivate this natural ability to play the piano. It is a gift."

Nicole felt like her heart was going to burst through the walls of her chest. *My idol is really praising my performance.*

"I would be much better if I could take lessons."

"Sometimes it is hard for a person who plays by ear to learn to play by note. A person who plays by ear puts so much more of themselves and their feelings into the music.

Not sure if she was ready to reveal her real identity Maxine turned the conservation to Nicole asking her about her family. "What sports does your brother play?"

Nicole was confused by the sudden shift of the conservation from music to her brother's sports. "He is an all-star soccer player and an all- state track star."

Maxine's thought flowed back to when John was ten years old. *John played soccer. Is his son following in his footsteps?*

Do I have a granddaughter and a grandson? Maxine thought. *I think they are part of the family I lost so many years ago.*

With a far- away look in her eyes Maxine sipped her coffee. After I graduated from the Carnegie School of Music, I began playing in night clubs. That's where I met Frank.

That is my father's name Kathryn thought taking a gulp of water. Kathryn wiped a tear from her eye. *Is Madam Maxine my mother? My father always referred to our mother as Maddie we never questioned what her real name was. When we asked about her, he would become terribly angry and say it was nothing we needed to be concerned with. We didn't know if she was living or dead. We had no pictures of her.*

Kathryn was only four years old, but she vaguely remembered her mother's disappearance. The longing for her mother created a dead spot in her heart. With no name there was no way to do a trace. Kathryn was too young to remember people who knew her mother.

That's probably why I never let anyone get close to me. I guess that's why I'm still single. And that's why I'm so protective of Nicole and Devin.

"When he returned from his third tour of duty in Viet Nam, he was a very abusive man, that night I did the most stupid thing I could have ever done in my life, I fled for my life and left my children in the care of a violent drunk.

"Please stop." Kathryn pleaded.

However, Madam Maxine continued as if she needed to let it all out. She swished the coffee in her cup, "the piano had been my voice, my expression, my life, without it and my children I felt empty and hollow."

The famous Madam Maxine appeared to be a lonely woman looking for a family to love and someone to love her.

"With five hundred dollars and a credit card in my purse, I hop a bus to New York City. But now it was time to come home."

Kathryn moved to Madam Maxine's side and pulled her close. By now she was convinced Madam Maxine was her mother. *But why did she just leave us? Why didn't she come back and get us?*

"John and Victoria will be back from his business trip later this week. I would like you to meet them." Kathryn said. "Will you come to dinner on Saturday?"

THE PIANO

"I would like that." Madam Maxine replied, delighted to have a chance to meet those that she thought were her lost children. Her heart was racing, she hugged Kathryn and Nicole, as they departed to their own homes.

I must get in touch with Ben and Luke Kathryn thought as she drove home.

Nicole was still floating on cloud nine as she let Madam Maxine's words roll over in her mind. "Madam Maxine seemed so sad." She said.

Kathryn didn't know how to explain to Nicole what she suspected. The family never talked about their mother's disappearance. *It might be better left unsaid until I know for sure.* She thought. "We may be able to cheer her up when she comes for dinner on Saturday."

Nicole went into the Parlor to practice. Madam Maxine's words had given her a greater determination than she had ever had before to become a concert pianist. *I will find a way to accomplish my dream.* She thought as her fingers flowed up and down the keyboard in the melody of In Shubert's Day.

Kathryn took out her phone and called her brother Luke. *I hope he answers.*

"Kathryn it's been awhile since we've talked."

Without even a greeting Kathryn almost shouted into the phone "I've an incredibly special person I would like you to meet!"

"The week of leave I put in for was just approved yesterday. It would be good to come home for a few days."

"John and Victoria will be here with Nicole and Devin."

"What about Ben?"

Kathryn hesitated for a moment, "I hope he will join us."

"It will be great to see the family. And I want to visit Dad at the Soldiers and Sailors home in Erie. Love you sis." *She was so excited, is my sister going to get married? "An incredibly special person?" Humm.*

Ben will be the one that will resist, Kathryn thought as she dialed his number. "Ben, I spoke with Luke and he is coming home for a visit later this week, John and Victory are stopping here for a few days on their way home from his business trip. Without taking a breath she continued. Nicole has been here with me the past two weeks and Devin will be joining us, I would like for you to come and have dinner with all of us on Saturday."

"Maybe some other time."

"Our family won't be complete without you." *Somehow, I have to convenience him that he needs to be here.* "Ben please come it's been more than three years since all four of us has been together."

CHAPTER 8

Convinced that Madan Maxine was her mother, Kathryn wanted every detail of the Saturday night dinner to be perfect. The thoughts of, *why did our mother never come back to get us? What was her life like in New York? Did she try to find us?* Kathryn wanted to go to the phone and call Madam Maxine and ask her all the questions that plagued her mind yet, she knew she must respect her privacy.

Not having a mother to teach her how to maneuver the kitchen didn't give Kathryn much desire to learn to cook and Living alone had never given her a reason to make it a priority in her life.

How am I going to serve a meal suitable for such an important event as this? As that thought fleeted through her mind the commercial on the counter TV announced the School of Culinary Art at the Pittsburgh Technical College. *That's it! I will call the school and see if they have students that can-do private dinners.*

Kathryn's feelings were a jumble of joy mixed with sorrow. *The lost piece of my life has surfaced but how will I handle it? How will my brothers react to it? I must find a way to convince Ben to join us for dinner on Saturday. I won't lie to him. I don't want to prematurely speak my feelings and have this all turn out to be a figment of my imagination just because I want so badly for it to be true.*

Nicole was at the piano in the parlor, she spent hours practicing, 'In Schubert's Day,' she had auditioned to play it as the background music for a skit her class had participated in at school, but another student was chosen. *I'm sure it was because that student had several years of lessons.* She thought.

This arrangement of In Shubert's Day made Aunt Kathryn's heart light. Smiling she entered the parlor, the flow of the music coming from the piano made her realize how lonely she was going to be when it was time for Nicole to go home. *When John and Victoria arrive, I will get to the root of his problem with music. Nicole must be allowed to develop her beautiful music talent.*

"Louise called; Kevin would like to come by and see you." Kathryn said.

"I want to see Kevin, but I must practice…" *there's that excuse again.* "I want to prove that I was worthy of Madam Maxine's words of praise for my music."

"You must relax and be yourself, and your music will reflect the true you."

When Louise and Kevin arrived Nicole and Kevin retreated to the porch. Aunt Kathryn brought the snacks and drinks she had prepared.

Relieved to have someone to express her thoughts, her hopes, and her fear too, Kathryn returned to the kitchen assured that Louise would listen and have some advice as to what she should do.

"Thank you for bringing Kevin by to see Nicole."

"Are you ok? You sounded upset on the phone."

"I've encountered a situation that I don't know how to handle."

"That is so not like you."

"This is something that is more like a fairy tale, than a real-life experience."

"I will help you in any way I can. Just tell me what is going on."

"I think Madam Maxine is my mother!" Kathryn blurted out.

"What has led you to that conclusion?"

THE PIANO

"So many things that she said and the questions she asked me when Nicole and I had dinner with her has caused me to suspect that she is my mother."

Louise sat stunned for several minutes before she quietly asked. "If she is?"

"There are twenty-five years of catching up..."

"If she isn't?"

"If she's not it was a wonderful experience just to have met her and for Nicole to have met her idol."

Over the years it was easier for Kathryn to pretend her mother had died rather than explain to her friends that her mother just left them. But she always hoped that someday she would find her.

Nicole was reluctant to share with Kevin the hurt and anger that was in her heart. Having won the top prize in the Children's Music Forum was clouded by what her father would say when he found out.

"I was only supposed to be here for two weeks," Kevin said, "but my coach has scheduled a couple of more soccer games for us to compete in, one on Sunday and the other one on Monday.

"My family will be here on Saturday; I would like you to meet them. I'm sure you and Devin will have a great time sharing your soccer experiences. He would probably like to come to one of your games."

"And you?"

"I would like to come."

"You said he was an all-star- player maybe my coach would let him play with our team."

Nicole quietly reflected on her inter feelings. *Why is it so easy for me to enjoy Kevin's success as a soccer player, but not want to be part of my brother's sports? Have I let the hurt of my father's devotion to Devin's activities overshadow my love for my brother? Am I jealous of my father's love for my brother? If only he could understand my love for music like he does Devin's love of sports.*

It was easy to talk to Kevin, but Nicole wasn't ready to open up and let him know why she could not pursue her dream of becoming a concert pianist.

"Hey, you still with me?" Kevin asked taking the last gulp of his drink. "We have a few more days, there is so much to see here in Pittsburgh, I thought we might do some sightseeing."

"What were your favorite things to see when you would visit your grandmother?"

"When I was young my grandmother would take me to the Carnegie Museum of Natural History to see the dinosaurs. As a little kid that was really cool. They have all kinds of activities and experiments to do there."

"That may be a fun thing to do."

"Another thing I really enjoyed was the Fife and Drum Corps at the Fort Pitt Museum but, that is only at the Fourth of July. There is the Buhl Planetarium. This is Mr. Rogers Hometown."

"Are you kidding! The Mr. Rogers from Mr. Rogers Neighborhood."

"That Mr. Rogers. His nearly 9,000 square foot home in the Squirrel Hill area of the city, where all his programs were filmed, is worth 1.4 million dollars."

"I loved Mr. Rogers, the music and that little train that came out of the tunnel at the beginning of his show."

"He was quite talented. He played the piano, sang, tried his hand at art and wrote and produced all his own show."

"Maybe it is time for me to consider doing some other things. Whatever I do has to complement my music."

"Finding some new interest may enhance your music and help you make new friends."

"Why does that sound so different coming from Kevin? Because he isn't mocking me, he is just suggesting that I can have more than one interest."

"What about drama?" Kevin asked.

"There is a lot of music in drama. Especially in the musicals. Kevin, you are such an inspiration to me."

"Our goal should always be to lift up and encourage others even if we don't have the same interest."

"I'm glad you nearly run me down in the airport."

"I'm glad my grandma and your Aunt Kathryn were friends."

"I never thought our paths would cross in a city as large as Pittsburgh."

"Me either."

"We are having a family dinner on Saturday; I'm sure Aunt Kathryn wouldn't mind if you and your grandmother would join us."

"Louise, I never took an interest in cooking. Living alone there was no need for me to learn." Kathryn sadly admitted. "I want this dinner to be something special."

"I loved to cook from the time I was in middle school. My mother was a wonderful cook and she taught me to make all kind of special dishes. We're Italian and her lasagna was the best."

"That's another problem I'm not even sure what nationality we are."

"You let me work on the food, you concentrate on getting the dining room ready."

Kathryn placed the china on the table. Should I order a fresh flower centerpiece?"

You have so many beautiful things," Louise said. "The gold candle holders and fresh flowers would add an elegant touch to this beautiful china."

"When I bought the house all these things, the furniture and accessories were part of the purchase. There were also linens and some beautiful quilts. I've never used the china before."

"Did the family not want any of it?"

"It was an estate and there were no living relatives. I think it was willed to a charity and they wanted to have the cash from the sell to promote their organization's projects."

The banquet table was large enough to seat twelve people.

"I would like you and Kevin to join us for this special occasion."

"This is a time for you and your family to re-unite, Kevin and I may make them uncomfortable."

"You are my Master Chef." Kathryn chuckled. "Nicole and Kevin have formed a friendship and he has awakened a new attitude in her."

"My hope is that Madam Maxine is who you think she is and that your brothers are receptive to accepting her."

"I'm going to need your support if my brothers don't accept her or that I find out she isn't my mother."

Louise made a check of the kitchen cabinets to see what kind of cookware was available for her use. "I will stop by the grocers on my way home and make the lasagna sauce tonight. Have you decided on dessert?"

"My mind has been in such a whirl. I've been rehearsing in my thoughts how I'm going to react to Madam Maxine if she is my mother or if she isn't."

"The best thing is to be yourself. People have always been drawn to your friendly outgoing personality."

"You're giving me the same advice that I have been giving Nicole about her music. I guess it's good to take your own advice."

"How does Chocolate cake with chocolate icing sound?"

"I've had a craving for chocolate these last couple of weeks."

"Chocolate cake with chocolate icing it will be."

"John and Victoria will be meeting up with Devin at the airport and they should be here by three o'clock." "I should be here about 10. I will drop Kevin off at the soccer field for his practice on my way over. That will give me plenty of time to put the finishing touches on our dinner menu."

THE PIANO

"You are a God sent." Kathryn said wrapping her arms around Louise's neck.

"I'm so glad we caught up with each other after all this time."

"And it was amazing that Nicole and Kevin connected in a city the size of Pittsburgh, after they went their separate ways when they got here."

"It looks like everything here is ready. I will see you in the morning."

Kevin and Nicole entered the kitchen. "Aunt Kathryn I would like for Kevin to come and meet Daddy, Mom and Devin. Would it be ok if he comes to dinner tomorrow night?"

"He and his Grandmother are already invited."

With a fist bump Kevin said, "See you tomorrow I have soccer practice in the morning."

That will give me practice time before Daddy, Mom and Devin get here.

Not sure how Kathryn and John would react to her, Madam Maxine's anxiety level rose as she contemplated tomorrow evening's dinner. *If only Ben and Luke could be there. With Luke in the Air Force, he is probably stationed somewhere away from Pittsburgh. Kathryn said she doesn't have much contact with Ben. At least this will be a start.*

CHAPTER 9

Kathryn's nerves were on overload as she and Louise began the final preparations for tonight's dinner. "I'm, so nervous about this dinner. partly because I want Madam Maxine's approval of me as a daughter, as much as Nicole wanted her approval as a musician."

"Just be yourself. For as long as I've known you, you have always attracted people to you by being yourself without putting on airs."

Nicole was already at the piano. *I must take advantage of this time before Daddy arrives, maybe after he meets Madam Maxine, he will be more receptive to my music.*

Kathryn took out her phone and dialed Ben's number. "Ben will you please come for dinner tonight." She begged. "John and Luke will be here,"

"I will come for a little while then I have things to do," Ben answered.

Things to do. Kathryn thought. *I need to make it a point to have more contact with him. I hope he hasn't retreated into depression again.*

When Devin, John and Victoria arrived from the airport, Nicole flung herself into her parents' arms, greeting Devin with a high-five. "I'm so glad we are all back together."

"I don't want us to be apart like this again." Victoria said. "I'm glad you had a good time, but I worried about both of you the whole time."

THE PIANO

"It was fun being at the lake with our cousins, but I'm glad we are all here now. I'm ready to go home and get to soccer camp." Devin added.

"I have a new friend; he plays in a traveling soccer league they were playing to raise money for the Cancer Center at Children's Hospital. His Grandma and Aunt Kathryn are friends."

Knowing that her father would be angry, Nicole could no longer contain her excitement. I participated in the Children's Music Forum, and I met my idol, Madam Maxine."

Victoria hugged her daughter. *Somehow her father has got to realize he has a daughter with interest different than her brother. She must be able to pursue her music talents just as her brother pursues his sports.* "That must have been exciting."

John hated the scars music had left on his life. *I know it is hurting my wife and my daughter, but music, especially piano music brings up all the bad memories of my childhood. I know using expensive vacations and gifts to compensate for this is not the answer.*

Throwing a sarcastic glance at Kathryn, John hung his head and said, "Is this why you wanted Nicole to spend the summer with you? Did you have this all planned before she came?"

"John, for once can you just see how talented your daughter is and how much music means to her. We need to have a talk about this."

"Some other time," John replied, returning to the car to get their luggage.

Kathryn's heart ached for her brother. All these years he has had something buried deep inside of him that has hindered his relationship with his daughter. *We must get to the bottom of this.*

"We are having a special guest for dinner tonight," Kathryn announced.

Concerned that Ben might not show up she went into the kitchen where Louise was putting the last-minute touches on the salad. "What if Ben doesn't come?"

"You have no control over what your brother chooses to do."

Madam Maxine arrived promptly at six. "Madam Maxine, this is my father John, my brother Devin and my mother Victoria." Nicole introduced her family.

"Luke! I wasn't expecting to see you." John exclaimed answering the door.

"Kathryn said she had a very special person she wanted me to meet. I thought she might be getting married." Luke chuckled. "Will Ben be joining us?"

"Hopefully," Kathryn replied. "He said he would come for a little while. Madam Maxine's heartbeat wildly. *Is this really happening. My children all together with me.*

"Uncle Ben is here," Nicole announced.

"Hey, Sis, when did you learn to cook?" Luke teased.

"I didn't, my friend Louise volunteered to be my master chef tonight."

Louise directed everyone to their seats on her carefully planned seating arrangement.

Around the dinner table the talk was about the week's events. John shared about the results of his business trip, while Devin and Kevin talked about soccer. Nicole talked excitedly about the places she and Aunt Kathryn had visited.

Madam Maxine sat quietly listening to the family share their events of the past few weeks before entering the conversation.

"John and Victoria, you have an incredibly talented daughter. Her performance at the Children's Music Forum was outstanding."

I won first place." Nicole interrupted, bringing her trophy from the piano.

John knotted up his fist and banged it on the table. "My daughter will do better things with her life than just play the piano."

Her father's piercing words cut a deep wound in Nicole's heart. Those words followed her as she grabbed her trophy and ran upstairs to her room.

THE PIANO

Finally, he let out all the hurt, anger and frustration that rose up in him over the music issue. "Our mother left us when we were young because she loved her music more than she loved us."

I hope my music never becomes more important to me than my family. Nicole thought, as she flung herself on the bed, drowning her hurt in a flood of tears. *At home I would have Snowball to cuddle with me.*

"I will never lay my fingers on another piano keyboard." She spoke to Madam Maxine's picture on the wall above her bed, throwing her trophy across the room. You were my idol and now you have become a wedge between me and my father."

Madam Maxine wiped the tears from her eyes. "Your mother fled for her life."

"How would you know that?" John shouted.

"This is our mother." Kathryn whispered.

"Our father always told us you left us because you loved your music more than you loved us." John stared at her, then Kathryn. What a resemblance. And Nicole could easily pass as Kathryn's daughter. "Why did you leave us and never come back?"

"When your father returned from the war, he was a very violent man. He did his first tour of duty in Viet Nam after you were born. When he returned, he was stationed state side for the next four years, during which time Ben and Luke were born. Kathryn was born while he was deployed for the third time. Four Children in six years."

They all sat in silence not knowing what to expect next.

"When your father was deployed for the third time, there were letters every week, sometimes twice a week, then once every couple of weeks. I dismissed the fact that the letters were less frequent because of where he may be in the country. Then the letters starting coming only once a month and then there were none. I didn't know if he had been captured or killed. Then he showed up at our door, drunk and incredibly angry."

John sat in shock. *Is this a dream or a horror movie?*

"After eighteen months of single parenting and working a full-time job I was drained. The stress of raising four children alone and giving up my music made me angry and resentful."

Nicole returned to the dining room and quietly slipped into her seat beside Madam Maxine. "I'm sorry," she whispered.

John's heart broke at the sight of defeat on his daughter's face.

"I left that night in fear for my life. Paralyzed with fear I walked the streets for hours. I don't know if I stepped out in front of that car, all I know is I woke up in the hospital. They told me I had been hit by a car. After I was released from the hospital I came home, and your father had taken you all and everything in the house except the piano and some of my personal things." Her voice cracked as she continued to relate to them the events of the next 30 years. "For years I searched for you. Each time I had a tip of where you were," she cleared her throat, when I arrived there, he had taken you somewhere else."

Everyone sat in silence not knowing what to say. After several minute Madam Maxine continued. "I put the piano in storage and went to New York City hoping to make it big on Broadway with my music. I never used my last name because I didn't want your father to track me down. I wasn't sure what he might do to me. For several years I played in clubs and bars and struggled to have a room to sleep in and food to eat."

"How did you become Madam Maxine?" John was still in shock. "How do we know you are our mother?"

"One night I was playing in a club when a man asked me to audition to play on some of the New York stages. Not wanting to use my last name I became Madam Maxine. My real name is Maxine Elaine Yaffa."

"Our father always called you Maddie. We never knew your real name. Anytime we asked about you he would get angry and say it was nothing we needed to be concerned about."

They all sat in stunned silence for several moments. Madam Maxine couldn't contain her excitement about finding someone with the same last name. "Yaffa is such an unusual name that when I saw Nicole's name on the list of entries, I knew I needed to inquire about her and her family. Kathryn and Nicole both have the traits of the Yaffa family. And John you have the same statue and good looks as Frank Yaffa who swept me off my feet all those years ago in that club in Pittsburgh where I was playing the piano."

"I hope you aren't thinking about taking our daughter to New York to perform with you."

"No, I'm retired now and will be moving back to Pittsburgh, where I hope to promote young people's music talent. I've rented an apartment in Greentree."

John sat in shock at what had taken place in the last hour.

"Once I found a post office box address for you father." She waited for a reaction from John. When he made no indication that he heard her, she continued. "I sent birthday cards, letters and holiday cards, but never received any reply. After a couple of years, my agent received a box in the mail from your father with no return address. It contained all the unopened cards and letters that I had sent you all, with a note that said, 'do not send any more cards, to us you are dead.'

Still in shock, "How did he find your agent and know that you were Madam Maxine?" John asked.

"I have no idea. Maybe he saw a picture and connected me to my agent."

John, Luke, Ben, and Kathryn sat in disbelief at what they had just heard.

"We never had any pictures of you." Kathryn responded. "The only picture I have is the one above the bed in Nicole's room. I ordered that off a website."

"When we would talk to dad about you, he would get angry and tell us it was nothing for us to be concerned about." Luke added.

Madam Maxine brought her tote bag to the table. "I made a treasure box for each one of you and put all those cards and letters in them. Each year on your birthdays and holidays I would add new cards. When I was packing up my apartment, I thought of discarding them, but I decided to keep them just a little longer in hopes that someday I would find you all."

John opened his mouth to speak but no words came out. *How can I ever repair the damage I've done to my wife and daughter by believing a lie all these years?*

CHAPTER 10

Louise cleared away the dinner dishes and returned to the dining room bearing plates of chocolate cake. Kathryn followed with a fresh pot of coffee.

Ben quietly entered the conversation. "I guess I'm the black sheep of the family, a loser."

"You pulled yourself out of a life of drugs and alcohol after you served your country in the Army." Kathryn commented. "Now you have a good job as a welder, I wouldn't call that a loser."

"Look at you and John, he went to college and became a successful businessman, you're a doctor, Luke followed in our father's footsteps and made a career in the Air Force, and I guess my mother is a famous pianist."

"I'm the biggest loser in this family. If I can consider myself part of this family." *As much as I want this to be true, I must not assume that they are going to welcome me back into their lives.* "Welders are very important to our work force. Especially here in Pittsburgh, the city of bridges and all the new construction at the hospitals and universities."

"How could you be a loser?" Ben questioned. "You performed on big stages under the Neon lights."

"Those performances were always tarnished by the fact that my life was empty and meaningless without my children. My mind was plagued with the memories of the night I left you all with a violent drunk. That night haunted me. I tried to console myself by believing that what he did to me, he would never do to our children. He loved you."

Kathryn's longing for her mother had created a hard place in her heart that would never let anyone get close to her. *I guess that's why I'm still single. Now here she is.*

"I will not be offended if you cannot accept me into your lives." Maxine paused. "I know this has been quite a shock to you all and I don't expect you to just act like none of this took place."

"There is just so much to take in…" Luke said.

"We want to spend some time with you. We can't recover what was lost but we can build new relationships." John added.

"If we focus on the past, we have no future." Kathryn added. "Let's just start with today."

Maxine reached for her tote bag. These are the treasure boxes I made, they may not mean anything to you, but… she said as she took the first box decorated with replicas of Strawberry Short Cake, out and placed it in front of Kathryn. "you were obsessed with the Strawberry Short Cake dolls and accessories."

"I still have a few of them. I don't know how I managed to save them with all the moving around we did."

"I am so proud of you and what you have accomplished."

The tension around the table mounted. Kevin went into the kitchen to help his grandmother with the dishes. "There are enough tears flowing around that table to wash all these dirty dishes." Louise said.

"I don't know what I would do if my parents told me I couldn't play soccer anymore.

"There's so much healing that needs to take place in this family and tonight it has started."

"I hope Nicole's father will let her play the piano. She has such an amazing talent."

"Ben, this one is for you. You always liked building things with Legos. You had an erector set and you would build bridges and buildings." She said taking out a box with pictures of bridges located in Pittsburgh. "It's no surprise you are a welder that helps build those structures for real."

If I never play the piano again it could not compare to growing up without our parents, she thought.

"Luke, I can't believe how your statue is so much like your father's. I'm sure in your uniform you would sweep some young woman off her feet just like your father did me. You always loved planes. When you were in second grade, we took you to the Wright Patterson Air Force Museum in Dayton, Ohio. That day you said, 'Someday I'm going to fly one of them big birds.'"

Luke moved to Maxine's chair and put his hands on her shoulders. "That confirms that you are our mother. I remember that day. That memory played a part in me joining the Air Force."

Maxine handed him a box with a picture of the Memphis Bell on it.

"I had planned to go there this trip, but I would like us all to go see Dad at the Soldiers and Sailors Home in Erie Monday."

"Kevin has a soccer game Monday morning." Devin said. "He plays in a traveling league and one of his teammates had to go home. He asked his coach if I could substitute. The coach wants me to come by tomorrow afternoon so he can observe my soccer skills."

"I told Kevin that I would come to his games." Nicole added.

"I've never seen any of Devin's games" Kathryn said. "I would like to go."

Louise entered the dining room. "The kitchen is all back in order. Kevin and I will be on our way."

"What time is the game on Monday?" Luke asked.

"It's an early one because it is our last game, and the team will be heading home." Kevin answered. "The game is at eight in the morning. It should be over by ten."

"You will be leaving on Monday?" Nicole asked disappointed.

"The team will be leaving, but since I'm visiting my Grandma I will be here until Friday."

"If we all go to the game that would give us time to go see Dad. It takes about two hours to get to Erie." Luke said.

Maxine's heart yearned for all the years she had missed interacting in her children's lives.

"John, I haven't forgotten you," she said taking the last box decorated with mathematic equations, from the tote bag. "You were the mathematician."

There was no doubt in any of their minds that Madam Maxine was their mother. All the things she said about each one of them was true. No one could just come up with that information.

"John you look so much like your father and Devin looks just like you. Ben you favor my family and Kathryn, and Nicole are a combination of both families but they favor the Yaffa family more."

Kathryn ran her fingers around the edges of her box. "I think I would like to look at these in a quiet time alone."

"It's been an exhausting evening; I must call a cab." Maxine said folding her tote bag.

"I will drive you." Ben said, "I'm going that way"

With hugs, tears of joy for the new experience and tears of sadness because of the lost years, everyone said goodnight.

Kathryn took her treasure box and retreated to her bedroom. Her heart beat wildly in her chest as she opened the box. *Will this connect some of the lost pieces of the past.* She took out an envelope that was post marked a few days before her sixteenth birthday. She opened it carefully as if she expected something to jump out at her.

This is a very difficult day for me, she read. Today you will be sixteen. I missed tucking you in at night, I've missed your first date, your first kiss, your prom, your…Kathryn could not read another word through her tears. Exhausted she laid her head on her pillow and cried herself to sleep.

THE PIANO

The treasure box on the bed greeted Kathryn as she opened her eyes. She picked up the letter and finished reading it. *I will miss your wedding if you get married.* She continued reading. *I would give my life to undo what happened. I just want you to know that I've never stopped loving you and hope that someday I will see you again.*

Kathryn washed her face and dabbed on some concealer to hide the puffiness under her eyes.

In the quiet of the morning, with everyone else asleep, John poured himself another cup of coffee to clear the brain fog of what had taken place last night. *I have believed a lie so powerful that it has robbed my wife and daughter of the music within them.*

"It will be strange to have someone to call Mother after all these years." Kathryn said pouring herself a cup of coffee. "She must have carried a sadness within her that the bright lights of Broadway could not extinguish."

"That is strange, I can't image my life without Nicole and Devin."

"That is something we need to talk about. You must let Nicole develop that magnificent music talent."

"At the top of my priority list is repairing the damage I've done to my daughter."

"Not only her music. We need to talk about her school."

"A lie has stolen so much from our family."

"Because of your reaction when she talks to you about her music, she is afraid to talk to you about her school."

"She had become withdrawn this year in her new school. That jolly laugh that had always been a part of her even as a baby no longer fills our lives."

"Public schools don't have the same educational standards as private school and if you're not involved in sports you don't fit in."

"I emersed myself in Devin's soccer because it reminder me of the only happy memory I had of my childhood. When we moved so often, I could no longer be part of a team."

"The damage is not beyond repair. You must let Nicole know that you are proud of her accomplishments. It is amazing that she developed her talent to this level without a piano."

"That is all going to change as soon as we get home."

Wrestling with the emotions that welled up in him, he knew there was only one thing to do. *I must show my daughter I am proud of her.*

"Kathryn, I need your help."

"My big brother needs my help?"

Ignoring the tone of her voice, John poured out his heart to her. "We always celebrate our special occasions at our favorite restaurant at home, but this cannot wait until we get home. It will be so much better with all of us here, and her idol. Would you ask Louise and Kevin to plan a party for Nicole while we go to see Dad on Monday?"

We need to invite Maxine's friend Mr. Roberts. He was so impressed with Nicole's performance at the Children's Music Forum."

"Because of a lie I have destroyed my daughter's passion and her dream but by the truth it will be resurrected."

"I am so glad you have been set free from the turmoil that has held you hostage all these years."

"Tell Louise to spare no expense" John said handing Kathryn a credit card.

"You are my enemy," Nicole said pointing at the piano as she walked past the parlor on her way to the kitchen.

"I'm sorry," John said taking Nicole in his arms.

"It's ok Kevin has made me see that I need to pursue some other interest. Aunt Kathryn will you drive me and Devin to Kevin's soccer game this afternoon?

John's heart ached at his daughter's rejection. *Has this been how she has hurt because I rejected her music?*

CHAPTER 11

"I needed that break yesterday to simulate all the craziness of these last few weeks." Kathryn said. As she and Victoria had a quick cup of coffee before it was time to go to the soccer game.

"Saturday night did take a turn that none of us could have predicted." Victory responded.

"Seeing my mother again was something I had stopped hopping for a long time ago, and John being set free from the turmoil that has plagued him all these years…"

"I've tried to understand John's refusal to let Nicole pursue her music. As an adult I was able to accept his objection and fill my life with other things, but I wasn't into my music like Nicole is. I enjoyed playing my harp. Occasionally I would play it when John was out of town or at work. All Nicole ever wanted was his approval and to know that he was proud of her."

"That will all change tonight."

"What do you mean?"

"John has asked me to have Louise and Kevin plan a party to celebrate Nicole's trophy tonight. They will get it all ready while we go to see dad."

Nicole's alarm startled her. "I haven't been up this early since the last day of school." she said, quickly changing into the t-shirt with Kevin's team name on it and a pair of shorts. Nicole joined her mother and Aunt Kathryn in the kitchen. "Are you ok sweetie?" Victoria asked.

"I feel sad, today it's Kevin's last soccer game," Nicole responded. "He will be leaving in a few days and we probably won't see each other again."

"It will be a fun game. Kevin's coach has let Devin be their substitute player."

"And Madame Maxine, *I hope someday I will be able to call her Mom,* asked if she could meet us there to watch the game." Kathryn said.

"It was nice having a friend who appreciated my interest even though it was different from his. I'm going to miss him."

"Once you get home your paths may cross like they did when you got to Pittsburgh." Victoria comforted her.

"We met here because Aunt Kathryn and his Grandma were friends."

John was on the sidelines cheering for Devin and Kevin. "Come on guys you've got this one."

"We need to sit in the middle, so we can see both ends of the field." Nicole said as they made their way through the crowd.

Madam Maxine joined them. "John was always dribbling a soccer ball. He started playing when he was four years old." she said.

"I think he started teaching Devin to dribble the ball from the time he learned to walk." Victoria replied.

John ran up and down the sidelines shouting plays to Devin and Kevin. The coach approached him. "Sir I am the coach. I know you want your sons to play their best, please take a seat."

John made his way to where Kathryn, Victoria, Nicole, and Maxine were sitting. "That man on the other side of the field is a member of the Riverhounds"

"Who are the Riverhounds?" Maxine asked.

"They are Pittsburgh's professional soccer team."

For the first time Nicole actually enjoyed watching her brother play soccer. *Oh, if Daddy would only show just a little interest in my music.* She thought.

THE PIANO

"Did you see Louise?" John asked.

"I think she was helping at the concession stand." Kathryn replied.

"Is everything set for tonight?"

"It's all good to go."

"Ben and Luke are going to meet us at Kathryn's house." John announced.

Kathryn questioned the van that was parked in her driveway when they returned.

"I borrowed my boss' seven passenger van so we don't have to drive two cars." Ben said.

Kathryn's apprehension about seeing her father increased as she and her brothers reminisced about their childhood.

"We moved so much," Luke said. "Sometimes it was sudden like Dad was running from something or someone."

"He would hold a job for awhile and then start drinking again." John added.

"Those actions were most likely flash backs from the war." Maxine's heart ached for her children. "During that war they sprayed a chemical known as Agent Orange to kill the vegetation, but it also killed people and left deep and lasting wounds and defects on those serving in our military."

"I've tried to prepare myself for the time that I might come face to face with your father again. Over the years the anger and hostility has deadened, *will seeing him cause it to rise up again?* I don't even know what to say to him."

"He probably won't know you. I keep in touch with the staff at the home, they say sometimes he doesn't even know who he is." Luke answered.

Frank sat in his silent world.

"How is Dad doing today?" Luke asked as he approached the nurse's station.

"Today he is very withdrawn. Some days he's angry and frightened and others he is content to sit and watch television, nap, or stare at the wall. There are days that he is in a faraway place."

Maxine felt a fiery dart pierce her heart at the site of Frank's body slumped in that wheeled chair. "Luke you are the image of your father it breaks my heart to see him this way."

It had been a few years since Kathryn had seen her father. She felt like she was meeting a stranger.

"Hi! Daddy she said placing her arm around his shoulders.

"Maddie," he said grabbing her hand, his face lit up, tears streaming down his face. "You came to see me."

John brought Devin and Nicole close to Frank's chair.

"Johnny, did you win your soccer game today?" He asked patting Devin on the back. "Kat, he said taking Nicole's hand, "you left your doll in the truck."

Luke motioned for Devin and Nicole to come to where he was standing. "Dad thinks you are John," he said to Devin and he thinks Nicole is Kathryn, he always called her Kat.

"Why did he call Aunt Kathryn Maddie?" Nicole asked.

"He thinks she is our Mom."

"Doesn't he know who you, Uncle Ben and Dad are?" Devin asked.

"Not today, what is going on in his brain is an ugly disease that takes away the capacity for a person's brain to relate to things in the present, they live in the past, that's why he thinks you are John and Kathryn."

"I think he still loves you," Luke said pulling Maxine close. "Did you see how his face lit up when He thought Kathryn was you."

"I certainly wasn't prepared for this. Even through all the heartache and pain he put me through it breaks my heart to see him this way."

"There was nothing you or any of us could have done to keep this from happening."

THE PIANO

"My loss was great, but his loss far exceeds anything that I went through."

"We all have lost, but we have a chance to recover, he will not have that chance."

They all gathered around Frank's chair to say good-bye. Showing no emotion, he lifted his hand to wave good-bye to them.

Everyone was lost in their own thoughts on the ride back to Pittsburgh.

"I should have…" Maxine began. "If I had stayed maybe I could have helped him through this.

"There are many should haves, could haves and would haves, but it is too late for that." Luke said. "It is time for us all to move on."

"Would it be ok for me to spend a little bit of time with you all before I go home?" Maxine asked.

"We would love to have you visit," Kathryn answered. She could not tell her about the party. It would spoil the surprise for Nicole.

Kevin brought the balloons from Louise's car.

Louise lowered the top on the baby grand piano, laid out one of the beautiful linens from the dining room and brought the cake from the kitchen.

"That cake with the music staff and notes could sing out the words, 'Congratulations Nicole.' Kevin said. "It's beautiful."

Nicole squeezed her father's hand. *After what I witnessed if I never play the piano again, I will have my family* she thought. *That is more valuable than anything else in this world.* "That was so sad." She said.

"I will return the van to my boss and come back." Ben said pulling into Kathryn's driveway.

With a heavy heart Nicole excused herself. On her way upstairs to her room, she noticed the oak pocket doors to the parlor were closed. *That's ok, I don't want to see that piano anymore.*

Nicole lay back on her bed. *My idol is my grandmother, I don't know if I should call her grandma without her permission, and my grandpa thinks I'm his daughter Kathryn, and Devin is Dad, how much weirder can this get.*

"Everything is ready," Maxine announced. "Where is the guest of honor?"

John took Victoria's hand. "Nicole would you please come down here?" He called from the bottom of the steps.

"In a minute."

Kevin opened the large oak doors to the parlor and the guests gathered around John and Victoria.

Nicole appeared at the top of the stairway. "We are all waiting to hear you make that piano sing." John called to her.

Confused, Nicole froze. Mr. Roberts, Madam Maxine, Kevin, and his grandma.

"Tonight, we are celebrating your Trophy."

Overcome with the emotions that she had kept locked inside her, Nicole sat down on the steps, tears streaming down her face.

John joined her, "This night is all about you and your music."

"Come," Maxine invited her. "Give us that beautiful rendition of Chopin's Nocturne."

Mr. Roberts, Louise, and Kevin joined the family around the piano.

Nicole, let all the music that had been pent up inside her flow through her fingertips the piano keys.

"This young lady has a future in the music world. Maybe a professor at Carnegie School of Music. Mr. Roberts complimented her. "Music will enhance whatever you choose to do in life."

"It has been wonderful having our whole family together, and celebrating this special event with our new friends," John said, acknowledging Mr. Roberts, Kevin, and Louise, Sadly, we all will be going our separate ways in a few days.".

"The only thing that would have made it more complete is having Dad here." Luke said.

THE PIANO

"We need to plan a time when we can do some sightseeing." Kevin said to Nicole giving her the first piece of that beautiful cake.

"There isn't time for that now," Nicole replied. "You are leaving on Friday and I'm going to go home with my parents. Our paths may cross in Charlotte."

"I don't live in Charlotte."

"Oh!"

"I live in Raleigh. I will be going to High School there and playing for the school soccer team. I'm taking a break from the traveling team to concentrate on my senior year of high school."

"John commanded everyone's attention, Because of a lie that I let consume me, I destroyed my daughter's passion for her music. Sports are for some, but for Nicole it is music."

Kathryn's heart soared. *My brother has finally been set free.* She thought.

"Meet the next Madame Maxine!"

John pulled Victoria into his arms sobbing he buried his face in her hair. He reached for Nicole. "I'm so sorry for the bitterness I let a lie create in me."

Nicole and Victoria wrapped their arms around him.

"When we get home, sweet pea," he had not used her nick name in a long time. "We are going to go shopping for the grandest baby grand piano we can find."

Maxine brushed her tears away. "I would like Nicole to have my baby grand piano, I had to put it in storage, but I would rather see a talented musician like Nicole make use of it."

"Thank you, grandma! Nicole shouted throwing her arms around Maxine's neck. "I hope someday I will play it as good as you do."

"You will have the best teachers in Charlotte," John continued. Victoria, my dear your harp will be right in the living room with Nicole's piano. The two of you bring beautiful music into our home."

More tears, Louise thought. *The healing in this family is truly happening.*

"Through one person's music our family was divided," Madam Maxine said as her tears flowed. "And through one person's music our family is united."